BOSSLADYSHIP: COLOR ME A BOSSLADY

DR. SUE SPEAKS

ONYX PUBLISHING

First published in 2020 by Onyx Publishing, an imprint of Notebook Publishing of Notebook Group Limited 20–22 Wenlock Road, London, N1 7GU.

www.notebookpublishing.com

ISBN: 9781913206376

Typeset by Onyx Publishing of Notebook Group Limited.

BOSSLADYSHIP:
COLOR ME A BOSSLADY

A GUIDE TO HELP women, and especially women of color, to navigate a path to leadership and professional and entrepreneurial success.

This book is geared towards helping women who are both seeking to take on leadership roles within organizations, as well as those wishing to start their own business or grow their current business.

CONTENTS

FOREWORD

S O, I'M HERE, WRITING a blueprint for women of color. How did this journey begin? Well, that's a pretty interesting story: back in 2008, I began my road to a doctoral degree. In 2011, I would take a detour on this journey and do some sightseeing and daydreaming before getting back in the car and on the highway, always striving toward completion. The topic of my dissertation was the role mentorship played in black/African-American women achieving leadership, and it was in 2015, when I defended my dissertation, that I left the door open to the next woman to take up the mantle and actually create a blueprint toward achieving leadership.

Five years later, here I am, finally ready to continue on the note my dissertation ended on. It took me a while, but hey, better late than never, right?

But then again, why now? Why pick up *this* book, considering all the other books that are out there about ladies achieving varying levels of becoming a boss lady? In this book, I will discuss how being a female impacts a woman's road to success—and, more importantly, the subtle nuances of how such success is impacted if you are a woman of color. Indeed, people of color (black and Latino) are expected to make up 55% of the US economy by 2025, and, of course, women of color will be a part of this group. It is, however, important to address the special circumstances behind this demographic.

Let's first establish the terminology I use in this book and how we need this word to become a part of the lexicon moving forward. In this book, I refer to leadership as BossLadyLeadership; this is because what we do as women is more than simply "leading". Leadership as a woman is different from that as a man, and it is because of this that people create unique spaces where we can grow and prosper. As you may be able to guess, women of color in particular have to form even *more* creative spaces, not only because we have to deal with a male-dominated structure, but also because we are considered to be the "other" in organizations; the ones who don't always quite fit the conventional mold.

I am influenced by all kinds of women, and it's because of this that I wanted to write something that a wide swath of women would find useful. However, as I lay in bed, looking through the many, many, many books out there aimed at women, I found that I was attracted to some and not others; some "spoke" to me more as a result of their higher focus on either my current reality or my desired future. In light of this realization, I then understood that in order for my book to "speak" to women in a similar way, it, too, needed to find its niche; a niche to which I belong, and to which I can provide some useful information concerning how to achieve the goals my female readers have established for themselves, or spaces they wish to occupy. I am using my own unique journey (as well as the contributions of 20 other women of color) as the blueprint for this journey for my sisters of color. I have achieved my once-impossible goal of becoming a leader in a largely white male-dominated field, and I've also decided to become an entrepreneur (my side-hustle), which gives me a degree of credibility. Thus began this blueprint for creating a space for women to become BossLadyLeaders.

While achieving BossLadyLeadership was the ultimate goal, I understood that my sisters of color were facing an uphill battle and needed even more guidance than the other women I knew. With this in mind, my goal began to focus specifically on women of color (and all who identify as a woman of color) so that their concerns and stories could be shared. My overaraching goal in this was to create a community of support and growth for the women who were still in the ceaseless struggle so many women of color face in today's society.

As I created this blueprint for BossLadyLeadership, I wanted women of color to understand, first and foremost, that they were *not* crazy; rather, their #StruggleIsReal. As such, they needed to identify the areas of struggle, and then, accordingly, ways to both overcome these areas of struggle and achieve success as a result.

To do this, I've created a five-step process to achieving BossLadyLeadership, spanning from Chapter 2 to Chapter 6. I have incorporated a workbook into the blueprint of this book, meaning that once my sisters have completed the reading material, they also have the opportunity to work on the areas discussed and begin to create their own personalized success blueprint. If each woman spends time working through the activities detailed in each chapter, she will find that, at this book's conclusion, she is already equipped with all the tools, abilities, and skillsets required in order to achieve a) the goals that she sets out for herself; and, most importantly, b) the skills needed to ascend into leadership or successful entrepreneurship—whichever she determines is the path for she wishes to pursue.

The book begins, however, with introspection and exploration for the reader so as to first better understand who they are, including their strengths and weaknesses, before then presenting a series of activities to aid in defining exactly how to ultimately create a leadership and/or entrepreneurship reality.

In order to ensure the material is coming from a point of reality and validity, I asked several women of color to complete a survey about the items that are of chief concern in this book:

1. Do they perceive themselves to be a woman of color?
2. How has this impacted them professionally?

3. How does their culture impact their professional and entrepreneurial lives?
4. Would they be willing to offer snippets that could be shared in the book?

Another goal of this book is to include and validate the experiences of all women of color; this is to facilitate for the creation of a blueprint of success. Some of the insights shared by these ladies will be scattered throughout the book, too.

What I found intriguing about the survey was how many of these women shared similar experiences, something that served to convince me that this was a fairly universal issue that women of color experience. It is important to both share this information with other women of color, as well as to find ways to create a new reality in this new decade. While women of color tend to experience a great number of indignities, this book is not created to pander to any feelings of annoyance, but, rather, to *validate* their feelings, and, more importantly, show them how to overcome those issues and still have success—and even use their "differences" to their advantage!

We have recently seen in the news that California has put legislation in place to prevent women of color from being discriminated against if they choose to wear their hair in a natural style (e.g., braids; twists; afros; locks; etc); let's stop and think about that for a moment. For years, women of color were routinely expected to make their hair more Caucasian if they wished to be considered as "professional" and move up the corporate ladder. In essence, they were told that they could not be their own authentic selves: that was not valuable.

I, myself, have been a victim of this: I never wore my hair in any style other than straight, as I knew that if I wished to even have a place in the corporate boardroom, there were rules to follow. In December 2017, however, I opted to wear my hair in a natural style: I was going to Europe, and didn't feel like lugging a flatiron with me on a flight. Fortunately, my decision to do this did not create a big issue in my corporate life, and since then, I've alternated between natural and straight styles. Think, however, about how the former narrative impacts the psyche of a woman of color; to be told she is not good enough as she is!

And this is just one example: for other women of color (especially our Latina sisters), discrimination and bias rears its head in the case of their voices possessing a hint of a Spanish accent, or hair that is too dark and/or too curly. Women who are mixed or Asian also have similar levels of indignities, as they don't fit neatly into a box, and so are told they must conform in order to meet others' criteria for acceptability.

And here's the thing that we need to remember: yes, it would be utopia to live in a color- and culture-inclusive society, but that's *not the current reality*; rather, we live in a world that likes boxes, and wants everyone to both check a box and fit neatly into one. It's the reason behind why that survey with those 20 women I mentioned before became critical for me. It allowed me to see how women of color classified themselves; while there are few races, there are a number of ethnicities, and the distinction between color and ethnicity is as important to women of color as it is to those of Irish or Italian descent.

Here in the US, we ask people if they are a) black, or b) African-American, and sometimes, we lump those two together. Another favorite is if they are a), Hispanic/white, or b) Hispanic/black. Much to our dismay, there is always a box. What was important to me, however, was how these women of color viewed themselves. This is largely influenced by the fact that while I self-identify as black, I do not identify as African-American—yet when asked to check a box, I often need to make a decision that may not fall within the parameters of how I actually self-identify. Hence, like the good researcher I was taught to be, the survey sought to provide a framework of who these women were that I would be talking to.

Before we dive into the body of this book, let me first just admit to my own inherent bias prior to beginning writing it: I, at the time, only really viewed black and some Latina/Hispanic women as "women of color"; however, after the research that went into this book, I was amazed at how many women of mixed heritage, as well as those who were Asian, also considered themselves to be women of color. My bias was further brought into sharp view when Andrew Yang, a 2020 Presidential candidate, referred to himself as a person of color. In my mind, he was Asian, and that was a different category altogether; however, his definition of himself helped confirm for me that all of us women who are *not* part of the white majority do experience leadership and professional life differently than that of our white sisters, thus necessitating a different kind of understanding and path to leadership.

Survey Results

20 women were surveyed; these are the results.

If women of color are women who are part of the Black diaspora, African-American, Hispanic, Latina, Asian, East Indian, Mediterranean or Native American, do you consider yourself a woman of color?

20 responses

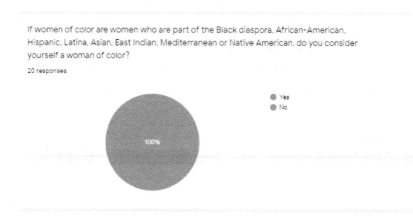

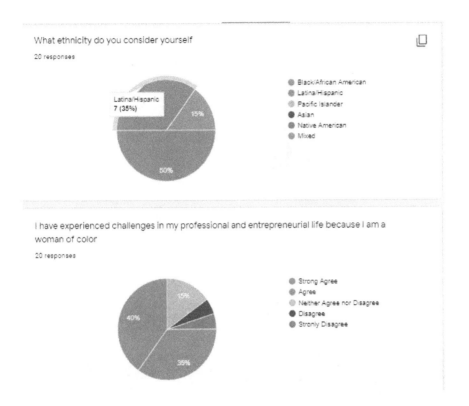

What ethnicity do you consider yourself

20 responses

- Black/African American
- Latina/Hispanic
- Pacific Islander
- Asian
- Native American
- Mixed

Latina/Hispanic
7 (35%)

15%

50%

I have experienced challenges in my professional and entrepreneurial life because I am a woman of color

20 responses

- Strong Agree
- Agree
- Neither Agree nor Disagree
- Disagree
- Stronly Disagree

15%

40%

35%

As a woman of color, do you feel pressure to be professionally successful by those in your ethnic group or culture

20 responses

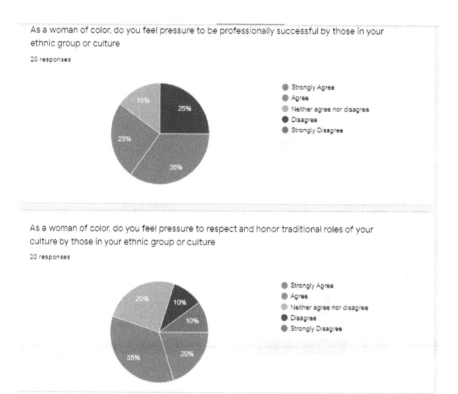

- Strongly Agree
- Agree
- Neither agree nor disagree
- Disagree
- Strongly Disagree

As a woman of color, do you feel pressure to respect and honor traditional roles of your culture by those in your ethnic group or culture

20 responses

- Strongly Agree
- Agree
- Neither agree nor disagree
- Disagree
- Strongly Disagree

Imposter Syndrome is defined as a collection of feelings of inadequacy that persist despite your being successful. Those who suffer from Imposter Syndrome suffer from chronic self-doubt and a sense of intellectual fraud that override any feelings of success despite evidence of your competence to others. Do you feel you have you ever experienced Imposter Syndrome?

20 responses

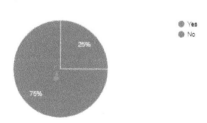

- Yes
- No

You experience self doubt in your abilities to be successful because of the comments and actions of friends or family of the same cultural and/or ethnic background

20 responses

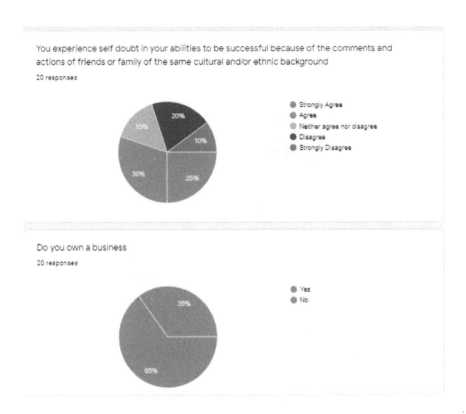

Do you own a business

20 responses

It was difficult to start my business

20 responses

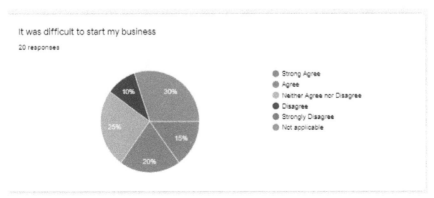

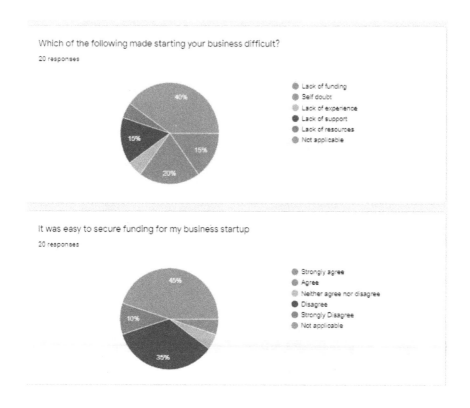

Which of the following made starting your business difficult?

20 responses

- Lack of funding
- Self doubt
- Lack of experience
- Lack of support
- Lack of resources
- Not applicable

It was easy to secure funding for my business startup

20 responses

- Strongly agree
- Agree
- Neither agree nor disagree
- Disagree
- Strongly Disagree
- Not applicable

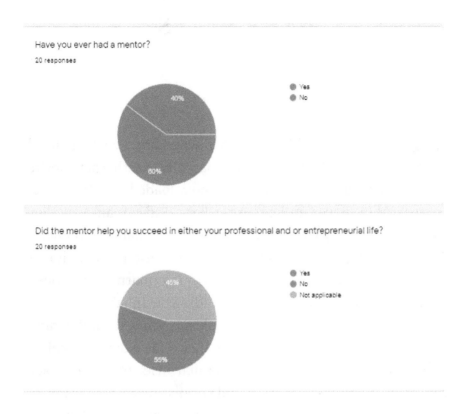

Have you ever had a mentor?

20 responses

- Yes
- No

40%

60%

Did the mentor help you succeed in either your professional and or entrepreneurial life?

20 responses

- Yes
- No
- Not applicable

45%

55%

These survey results provide a backdrop to some of the stories and commentaries that will be included in this book.

CHAPTER 1:
BABY STEPS

WHEN SOMEONE ASKS ME who I am, I cock my head to the side, wondering what it is exactly that they're asking me. I find this to be a loaded question, and, in turn, I'm never quite sure what kind of answer they expect—especially when asked in a professional environment. Are you asking me about my job; my education; my heritage? As an immigrant woman of color, my journey has been different from other women of color who inhabit the same space that I do; saying this, it took me *years* to understand that, while my journey was different, we (as women of color) all inhabit the same space, have similar insecurities, and face the same prejudices and trials and tribulations. This means, of course, that we need to embrace the successes and joys of others so that we can progress as both women and women of color.

Here's the thing though: how do you do that? How do you bond with other women of similar backgrounds? How do you share your experiences with others? How do you learn from other women that you are unlikely to meet in your day-to-day life? How do you benefit from the collective knowledge out there? And, more importantly, how can you share those insights you've gained on your journey with others? How do you pay it forward?

I ask all of these questions because what I knew for sure was that where I stood then, at that very moment, was because of the many women who'd passed through my life: women who had shared insights with me; women who had supported me; and even a few women whose disdain or disregard had spurred me to prove myself even more.

Now, I found myself wanting to connect and share with such women more and more; I wanted to be a catalyst for change for other women. I'd had some experience, formally and informally, in mentoring women of color to achieve professional goals—but *now*, I had an urge to do this on a more global scale. I'd seen the explosion of a variety of women's movements and realized that I, too, had something valuable to add to the conversation.

So, what do you do when you realize that you have a question?

You ask them.

I began verbalizing my want to find a way to bond with and help more women to a core group of female friends and colleagues, and, sure enough, they all responded to me with the same notion: you're an educator, so do what educators do: educate, and write a book!

A book? Cue my panic!

I've been an educator for over 20 years, and that was something I fought tooth and nail. When my college aptitude assessment stated I should be a "teacher", I was highly affronted. A *teacher*? Not me. My goal was to be a professional career woman—and yet what I didn't seem to realize was that education could be such a professional career for me.

For years, people have told me I should write a book. The first time I was told this was when I was working as an Internet marketing teacher. In the early 2000s, when people first began to realize the power of the Internet, there was no Internet marketing textbook—and so I was literally teaching based on the guerilla marketing tactics that we used in real-time in the industry. Notably, it was the porn industry that was leading the charge—so imagine me as a teacher, sanitizing porn strategies to help students learn how to market their grandma's church!

Because I was using some of my own strategies to create lesson plans, some of the faculty told me to take my notes and simply collate them and write a textbook using my own materials.

At 29, I was too young and inexperienced to understand the value of such a suggestion; being an author or creating that sort of reality was not on my radar, and I felt that I didn't have enough experience or enough of a voice to warrant my taking on such a challenge. Truth be told, I was also going through other self-growth challenges at that time, and felt I was too busy just with keeping it together to add such a challenge to the list.

It was two years later that I saw a guerilla marketing textbook in the bookstore, and it was then that I did pause for a moment and wonder if I'd made a mistake.

That was the first time I'd understood the power of taking advantage of something when it is presented to you; the power behind *always* lunging for an opportunity. After all, you never know how that opportunity could manifest itself for you.

Years later, I would hear about NaNoWriMo, a scheme that challenges writers to write 50,000 words between November 1st and 30th—1,666 words a day. I took up the challenge in 2011—remember, I'd learned to never ignore a challenge when offered at that point!—and wrote a romance novel in the process. I ended up having the personal joy of knowing that I polished off 65,000 words in 30 days.

Now, you may ask, "How did you do this?" Well, I'd begun a doctorate in 2008, and so had developed a rhythm for writing on a daily basis: I'd completed my comprehensive exams, and was taking a brief hiatus before beginning my actual dissertation. Thus, instead of coming home and researching leadership strategies and organizational dysfunction, I simply wrote about the romances I'd seen on TV, read about, or experienced.

Once I completed the challenge, I saved the novel and went back to the task of dissertation-writing, happy in the knowledge that I'd conquered the challenge. While writing, I had, however, toyed with the idea of seeking out a publisher and seeing if there was any interest, but the idea never ever took solid root. This disregarding of such an idea did not prevent a seed from being planted, however; it would later serve as another link in the chain that has led me to this point of writing this book. Eight years later, I would take up the same challenge again to write a book and take it to its natural conclusion: successful publication and distribution.

Now, I find myself at an interesting point in my life: I'm looking at all these disparate pieces and trying to put them all together into a logical puzzle. An evaluation of my professional life thus far presents a need to determine whether I'm going to continue in the same career, or make a shift—and if I *do* shift, where I would go. Where would my skills and knowledge best be used? Should I become an employee again? Or should I branch out of my own? Coupled with such professional questions are questions of whether my son will go away to college soon, allowing me to experience the joy of an empty nest. My marriage is also shifting from the loving union we've shared for nearly 20 years, to something else that is yet to be defined.

Everything is shifting, and the only thing I have any control over is myself. With this conclusion reached, I decided to invest heavily in myself and my growth over the next 18 months. It is, after all, a new decade; what better time to create a metamorphosis? Ordinarily, in the trajectory that has been my life, it's always been me guiding others when *they* get to these junctures in their personal or professional lives—so, in an interesting twist of fate, instead of being the mentor, I became the mentee.

One of my former students, who is 10 years my junior and who now works for me, began slowly urging me to make some changes. "You're a thought leader," they said, "so *be* a thought leader."

What would happen over the next six months was a slow evolution of me, my choices, my realizations, and my growth. As I was sifting through all these issues, my new mentor (let's call her Lulu, @socialwithlulu), through quiet reinforcement, simply shifted me to a  new reality. I'm still trying to figure out how she managed to maneuver me into doing all the things she did, but, regardless, she succeeded in single-handedly encouraging me to launch my business. Without her, I'm not sure that I'd have had the courage or impetus to do this—not, perhaps counterintuitively, because of fear of failure, but because I was spending a lot of time in introspection, pondering the issues and the what-ifs, rather than actually taking action. I also didn't think that with all the fabulosity out there that my voice could be heard or relevant above the din.

However, after many months of conversations, her words finally began to penetrate the chaos swirling in my mind, and I took a step forward. I first began toying with names on Instagram, and, in June 2019, I finally found a name I liked:

Dr. Sue Speaks. Then, on July 3rd, 2019, after somebody annoyed me at work, I shot a video and uploaded it to Instagram. That gave birth to my Instagram series, The Dr. Sue Speaks car videos. It was shortly after this that one of my staff members saw the video and asked me about my business. I sheepishly told him that I didn't have one, and he asked me why not. I told him that, with my full-time job, I didn't feel I had the time. He pinned me with a gaze and said, "The government gives you five years to have a hobby."

I got the message loud and clear. Yes, I may still have some lingering doubts, but hey: nothing tried, nothing gained. He had deftly removed all my arguments about timing, money, and possible failure. His words fired up something in me, creating a sense of urgency, and, within a week, Dr. Sue Speaks became an LLC. I got a website and, a few months later, a logo.

The journey had begun.

My student—now mentor—made it her mission to keep moving me forward at this point, quickly becoming the epitome of #WomenSupportingWomen. Mondays became her #MotivatonMondays for pushing me to new heights and systematically breaking through all my roadblocks.

This is a really critical story for all women to understand about BossLadyLeadership. I've been a leader in my professional life for over 15 years, but that didn't take away from the fact that I needed another boss lady to give me the gentle push I needed in order to take myself to the next level. The fact that I'd done that exact same thing for other women didn't mean that I didn't need some motivation and support myself. We'll discuss this notion of women supporting other women later, as nobody succeeds by themselves! We *all* need others to help and support us on our journeys.

I write and publish at least one academic article each year in order to stay relevant, force myself to keep abreast of trends, and satisfy ongoing professional development as part of the academic accreditation process. As my mentor Lulu put my website together, she pulled a few of my articles and added them to the site, too. She had decided that it was time for me to have a site, and before I could get cold feet about such a prospect, she simply created it for me.

2020 #BOSSBABE GOALS
BABES SUPPORT BABES

Now that I was branded on social media, her new push was that I needed to write a book for women before building an online learning module to teach women how to get to the level of success that I've enjoyed. I looked at her like she'd lost her mind, not because it wasn't doable, but because the speed at which she was looking at getting these things done was lightning fast. Me, the mentorship and leadership guru, had a head that was spinning!

When I told her this, all she did was smile and say, "It's

okay, we'll get there. Baby steps."

And, sure enough, the more I thought about it, the more the idea began to take root: not only did the idea of a book seem both realistic and doable, but the whole notion of creating a learning portal as a place where women could hone their skills and learn how to achieve success was beginning to make more and more sense in my own mind. As I commenced my research, I began to realize that this was truly something that I could do; and, with each passing day, it became something that I *wanted* to do. Women are natural collaborators, and I do well when collaborating with other women. It's also important to note that my Lulu is, herself, a woman of color.

The next chapter will discuss the first step in the process of how BossLadyship occurs: conducting a self-audit. While I've formalized the process here, this had been occurring for me over the course of a one-year period—and, as the chaos cleared and things began aligning to a strategic goal and action plans, here's what became crystal clear to me:

- I had already penned 60,000 words, so I knew I could manage the writing;
- I had already written a dissertation about the mentoring of minority women, so I already possessed much of the information on the topic;
- I had already mentored women of color;
- I had spent 20 years mentoring students and professionals to success;

- I was already (albeit informally) advising a plethora of women (of color and other) across a number of business platforms;
- In my professional life, I already oversaw online education and had created an online platform, so I knew how to create a solid, working online platform;
- I had already written policy and procedure, so I could certainly put together a manual for success;
- I had a network of women willing to support me to success.

I had all the raw materials required in order to make this book into a reality. However, it was not just writing the book that I realized had daunted me; it was the prospect of creating a whole new entrepreneurial direction for myself, in turn allowing me to help other women and pay forward the success that I've enjoyed over the last 20 years.

I decided that I would make this happen, but set no real timeline. Spoiler: this was a bad move! The Universe, however, has a way of correcting me when I don't commit to the designated path. One night, a few months later, a school friend asked me to help her get her book on the bestseller list by doing a pre-sale purchase. I bought it without a thought: my personal philosophy has always been, "If someone you know starts a business, then you support them." End of story. It was her closing line on her thank-you email that was prophetic: it simply stated, "You next!"

I suddenly realized that He was talking to me. I've always believed that we are never very far away from the things we need to know or do; we simply need to be calm and quiet and listen. Some people call it the Universe; I'm a woman of faith, so I know it is God guiding me to where He needs to me to be in order to accomplish what I need to accomplish. I've tried to listen to what He's asked me to do in life, and whenever I do, things seem to turn out fine. So, since He's leading me down this path, I'm going to follow it and see where it takes me; He's never led me astray. Saying this, I had to acknowledge that I still possessed some fear and trepidation at going into the unknown. Hence, I branched out in faith, remembering and holding onto the old adage that I had nothing to fear but fear itself.

It became a good time to remind myself that I'd written an article about F.E.A.R (False Evidence Appearing Real); I quickly realized I *had* to confront the issues creating some of my fear and angst. My employment was uncertain, and I was the chief breadwinner in the house. My personal life was in freefall, and I no longer had a status quo. The thing that this level of uncertainly created, however, was a need to both step out in faith and to step outside of my comfort zone. So, that was exactly what I did: stepped out. Comfort zone be damned! I couldn't be on social media posting about how "growth happens outside the comfort zone" if I was too chicken to put my money where my mouth was!

I did two things: first, I reached out to a resume expert on LinkedIn to discuss the possibility of making myself more attractive to hiring professionals, as well as to raise my LinkedIn profile so that I could begin to manage one area of stress: my professional life. While I wanted to pursue this book dream, I knew I had obligations, responsibilities, and bills to pay. Second, I coached myself out of my angst and began writing. I also found myself an accountability partner by sharing this with another fellow female entrepreneur (also a former student), who  would ensure that as soon as I came home every night, I started writing. At the end of the first night, I had written 5,800 words; I'd broken through Block One. I was excited, but this book would not be the first book I put out there; it would be the second.

Here's how you know when a plan is starting to come together: the next day, I called my school friend, Rachel R, whose book I'd just bought, to ask her who she'd used as an editor, as well as her process for being published. She then spent 30 minutes explaining to me how and what she'd done, and ended up sharing some of her personal journey with me. It was then that I realized that she and I were at exactly the same place in our journeys: she had begun hers exactly when I had begun mine. It began with the knowledge that something had to change, and that the time was now, and, while she and I share a cultural history (we are both Jamaican), she is not a woman of color.

I shared with her my idea of creating a blueprint for women to become #BossLeaderLadies. She loved the idea, and, to my utter amazement, she said to me that not only did I need to write the book, but that I needed to focus it on women of color. She also said that I needed to create an online learning platform to help women to fully understand and achieve their full potential.

I was sitting in my car with my phone on Bluetooth, my mouth hanging open. This was the second person telling me the path I needed to follow. The planets had aligned. Message received, loud and clear!

If I'd not believed before that He had a plan and was slapping me over the head with it now, I got it; He'd even allowed me to be dealt a devastating personal blow in regard to my job and personal life to even further galvanize me to get the ball moving! He ensured that He'd laid all the breadcrumbs for me, and had given me the time to get used to the path I needed to be on—and now, the time had come, and He was telling so. When the time is right to do something, you just know.

There was a sense of calm serenity that overcame me as I accepted this challenge, and, months later, when I began the publication process, the angst would return, as I was now investing monetarily in my vision. Spending large amounts of money is always scary!

I came home and wrote the book overview, made two pages of notes, and then waited two days to allow my thoughts to come together in a sensible, logical way. Then, on December 23rd, 2019, I sat in my bed with my laptop and started writing what I hoped would be both an entertaining, informative book for women of color, as well as all women who wish to realize their full potential and to create a path toward leadership and professional success.

So come on, ladies: let's get on it!

CHAPTER 2:
THE BEGINNING

I WAS BORN IN Jamaica, and I am descended from a variety of folk: black, white, and East Indian. I've been toying with doing an Ancestry DNA kit just to find out exactly what kind of Heinz variety mongrel I am! In Jamaica, there's never really a need to know all the details, but, while living in the US, I've begun to wonder exactly what the fabric of my DNA is comprised of; because boxes and labels are such a part of the cultural and corporate fabric.

In Jamaica, there is an obsession with attaching some races to one's ancestry; it creates a "prettier" skin tone or straighter hair, and, while it is a country whose population is 90% people of color, there is an unhealthy obsession with skin tone and hair texture. The country is now experiencing an epidemic of skin bleaching, a practice where both men and women use harmful chemicals to lighten their skin pigment, leaving permanent damage. Health and safety concerns aside, what this practice shows us is how pervasive the feeling that being a person of color is somehow something to be ashamed of and to fix is.

The reason for this is no different than any other culture: when those of affluence and privilege are lighter complexioned, there somehow seems to be more value placed on having a lighter skin tone or straighter hair—and, in a culture that sees the likes of Rihanna and Beyonce as the pinnacles of beauty, being lighter is seen as being better. I thought this was something that was only prevalent in black culture, but I would learn that this managed to permeate the Latino and Indian culture, too.

While the notion of beauty standards is not often seen as part of the discussion of how to be successful, it does go to the heart of self-confidence and self-worth: if a woman feels that who she is or how she looks is somehow not good enough, this can (and will!) erode that woman's confidence in herself, as well as her ability. Women of color must first learn to not just accept themselves, but to also *value* themselves and see themselves as beautiful, both inside and out. This, when done successfully, will serve as the first building block in any woman's success journey.

I remember thinking as a little girl that I was perhaps too dark in complexon. I cannot recall anyone ever saying anything to me directly to make me feel that something was wrong with me, but it was somehow in the ether. My mother did, however, tell me about one thing that occurred when I was a child: apparently, I had a teacher who made me stay back to clean the boards. I had no issue with it, but my mother certainly did: my mom had discovered that only the darker skinned children were ever given classroom chores, and so, unbeknownst to me, even at the tender age of seven, I'd been exposed to someone who wanted to treat me as less-than, simply because of who I was and how I looked—and in a predominantly black country, no less!

It took years for me to truly embrace and love my skin. I didn't hate myself, exactly, but it wasn't until I was in my late twenties that I remember looking at myself and really loving the person staring back at me in the mirror. I remember just sitting in front of the mirror and looking at myself: looking at my forehead, and appreciating it for being just the right size to wear my hair both in bangs and fully off my face; looked at the shape of my eyes and saw my grandmother's East Indian heritage; looked at my wider nose and the flare of my nostrils and smiled, because no amount of clothes-pinning had created that Eurocentric bridge. I appreciated the fact that each of my features were tied to one of my ancestors, and how it all came together to create me—and that that distinctive diastema (the gap between my front teeth that is now my logo) I had which was a family trait, existing in four generations (including my son), would set me apart from others. It was looking at all of these things and fully embracing them as quintessentially *me* that helped to solidify that I was fine just as God had made me, and that if I was changing anything, it was because *I* wanted to do it, and not to satisfy someone else's idea of who I should or need to be.

This is why I'm now so happy to see every moniker that's a homage to the celebration of melanin and black girl magic: our skin, noses, hair, the wide flair of our hip, the thickness of our thighs, and jut of our rear is something that we've been made to feel is not as good as a European standard. The things that make us unique are looked down on simply because they represent a different cultural ideal. Today, however, many young women of color have *finally* gained the representation in media and popular culture that they deserve, meaning our future generations will now be able to see themselves and their unique beauty. It is in this way that we can hopefully eliminate the idea that young women of color need to change how they look in order for their intellect to be appreciated. Their brain and intellect are housed in a unique vessel, and should not be used as either a cudgel to dominate or a yardstick to exclude. Women already have *enough* to contend with on a daily basis; adhering to a beauty standard in order to contribute to society does *not* be one of them.

I won't lie, though: while I understand that it was  essential that I underwent this process of self-acceptance, I'm not against surgery to fix things you don't like, or using products to make you better. While I love my diastema, I know two women of color who had surgery and wore braces to close theirs. For me, my diastema is a generational link to all those whom I am a product of, and not a flaw. For them, however, it was a distortion of their smile and how they wanted to see themselves. Both are beautiful, and if changing their smile made them happy, then I, too, am happy for them.

I am forever grateful for my mother and her obsession with good skincare—and mine in particular! I was not allowed to use soap on my face after the age of 11, and I had to cleanse my face with cold cream, toner, and moisturizer. I've continued her obsession, and for the 35 years that have followed, I have implemented a very rigid skincare regimen of cleanse, tone, moisturize—and now that I've discovered serums, I've added them to the list, too! Today, my skin is a thing of pride. Being a woman of color is a badge of honor I happily walk through life with. I enjoy my wrinkle-free skin even though I'm of a certain age, and I appreciate all the lessons that walking through life in *this* skin has taught me.

But why am I even talking about this? Well, my purpose here is to form some context around some of the things that we will explore as we move forward. The first is that I view the world and my feminism through the prism of being a woman, a woman of color, and an immigrant—and, while it may not seem like these things should make a difference, they do. As a Jamaican, I was raised in a largely matriarchal society, so my views on women, their roles, and how they should behave, will forever be colored by this. Further, Jamaica is a third world country that, unlike the US, has already had a woman lead the country. Hence, Jamaican men do not see woman leaders as an anomaly; rather, it's something they've come to expect and embrace. This is similar to the children who lived in Britain between 1979 and 1990 under the Prime Ministership of Margaret Thatcher: for those children, it was normal for a woman to be the head of government. After she left, it was seeing a man in charge of running the country that seemed unnatural, not seeing a woman in charge. When will we, in the United States, ever understand the unique qualities that a woman brings to leadership?

I moved to the United States at 19 years old to pursue a degree. It was not my plan to move here permanently, and I don't quite know when it was that I made the decision to stay, but it was during my years in college that I recognized that *my* reality and those of the people who were born and raised in this country were vastly different. This difference was neither good nor bad; it was just different.

We are all products of our environment. I'd been raised in a matriarchal society where women could achieve whatever they set out to do; one whose population was 90% people of color. Hence, people of color did not feel victimized or persecuted there—because they largely weren't! There was no systematic process of shutting us out of the process. So, after moving to the United States, it took me a while to understand the differences, as well as to garner an appreciation for the cultures of all the people of color who make up the fabric of the United States. More importantly, however, I came to understand that I needed to find my own place within that fabric.

There was an incident in college that I would not realize for years had triggered a slow evolution in terms of how I would operate professionally. I had been caught in the middle of an argument between a female student from the Caribbean and a female African-American student. The Caribbean student was being very dismissive and more than a little disrespectful of the role that African-Americans had played to achieve a somewhat level playing field for people of color; the African-American student, meanwhile, wanted her to acknowledge that she (the Caribbean student) was only here because African-Americans had fought to give her such an opportunity.

The Caribbean student went on to berate African-Americans, stating that they waited for everything to be handed to them. She said that that was why immigrants came and took what should be theirs: because they were too lazy and pathetic to get it. I found her comments more than a little disturbing: she was enjoying an opportunity to be in college as a result of other people fighting for her right to do so, and yet here she was, being extremely dismissive of that whole segment of history. They were enduring quite a détente, as neither party was willing to give in to the other's points. I remember it being a seminal moment in my understanding about what it meant to mediate, compromise, find middle ground, and how to get people to get on the same page.

I spoke to my island *sistren* and reminded her that we were standing on the backs of giants who had fought for us to be able to have a seat at the university—not only as immigrants, but as black people and women of color. I reminded her that it helped no one for her to not appreciate those who fought so that we could achieve. I then turned to my American friend and explained that, as immigrants, we had no expectations of getting anything, so we simply worked hard for everything we had so we didn't get the whole reparations discussion. I explained that what was needed was a discussion between both women so they could both better understand where the other was coming from.

It was evident that because my goal had been to bring each of these women to a greater personal understanding of the other's position (with the purpose of then usiing that understanding for growth), they both were quite annoyed with me. Looking back, however, I do believe that that was one of the many times when I used the skill of compromise and negotiation to try to build bridges. I didn't do much bridge-building that day, but I'd started down the road of learning how to have those difficult discussions where personal feelings are so embedded into the conflict that it's often difficult to even create a space for open dialogue.

The interesting thing is that I think that the person who learned the most from that encounter was myself: I understood that I needed to stand in the other's shoes before I ever passed judgment or made any decisions. It's a tool I use when mentoring, as well as managing and leading my own teams. Simply as a result of our personal histories, women of color have a unique ability to navigate these types of discussions; many of us understand that we are judged before people know who we are; that assumptions are made about us. We've had to learn that it's critical to learn all sides before jumping to any conclusions. This is a skill that should be harnessed, polished, and refined; it's quite a useful skill in corporate negotiations, after all!

The sad part in my memory of that discussion—something that happened over 25 years ago—is that it is still a discussion we are having today. People of color are still being systematically shut out of progress, advancement, and opportunities because of a system that does not always value them as individuals, their achievements, or what they bring to the table. As such, it is critical that *all* women of color, from *all* walks of life and experience, work to ensure a greater level of understanding and collaboration. This is with the greater objective of allowing for women to occupy a space of equality where their contributions and achievements are as valued as their male counterparts.

I got my two degrees and then marched into professional life. I didn't encounter any of the stark racism that many have in their career rise, and for that I count myself as fortunate and blessed. Now, don't get me wrong, it's not that I didn't experience *any*; I most certainly did. It's just that these instances were simply more veiled and unobtrusive than those of other women of color I've heard, and, in my naivety, I often didn't recognize it for what it really was. The first time I recall any overt racism was when I went to an in-person interview after having done a phone interview. I have a Jamaican accent, and so I assume for someone who's not familiar with it, it simply sounds British. I've been mistaken for South African on more than one occasion.

After an initial phone interview in which we agreed upon the job roles and pay, I went in to do an interview. This was after my masters, and so I was just dying to work anywhere so that I could pay my rent, car, and other bills. I would be earning a mere $30,000 as an Office Administrator, but it would pay the bills. So, I put on my best outfit and walked into the high-end realtor's office. You could have heard a pin drop when I walked into the office: I was clearly not what they were expecting! I watched the woman who'd been gushing at me previously find every way she could to backtrack, including using my degree to justify my being "overqualified". It was a tough pill to swallow, but I eventually understood that this was more about who I was than what I could do.

There have been, of course, several other smaller slights; if I had a penny for every time I've been complimented on how bright I am, or how well-spoken I am, I'd be giving Oprah a run for her money! The first couple of times, you appreciate the compliment—until you realize that there is an implied expectation that you are *not* bright, and are unable to pair a subject and predicate together to a logical conclusion. It is then that you begin to see the compliment for what it is: the very thinly veiled surprise that you, a woman of color, are as accomplished as you are.

This is the reason why I focused in on myself and how I'd gotten to where I was in life when it was time to pursue a doctoral dissertation topic. I finally settled on the field of education as my life vocation: I've worked as a Registrar, Faculty, Program Chair, Assistant Dean, Associate Dean, Faculty Development Director, Director of Education, Campus Director, Director of Online, as well as Vice President.

With all of these roles, I wondered how I managed to attain all of this: I was a Department Head at 30, an Assistant Dean at 35, an Associate Dean at 37, and a Vice President by 39. I honed in on a reason, figuring that what had fueled my meteoric rice was my mentorship by white men. I knew I had the ability and skill to do the job, but so did many others—so why had I advanced so quickly? I was convinced that the only reason was because of who had mentored me, and I spent two years of my life exploring this notion.

In my late twenties, I was working in the web industry. This meant I went to work in jeans, a t-shirt, and flip flops. A friend who worked in a more upscale Internet firm contacted me about a possible teaching job. Teaching? Really? But hey, a girl's got bills to pay and shoes to buy, so off I went to the interview!

Once there, I apologized for being inappropriately dressed, but he waved me off and told me it was fine. My interview concluded at 6pm that Monday evening, and I was handed a textbook and began teaching at 6pm the following Wednesday. If you're a teacher, you're probably grinning right now: so many of us began our teaching careers in this exact way (i.e., completely thrown in at the deep end). This began my career at the Art Institute of Fort Lauderdale, part of the now-closed Education Management System of Schools.

Steve, my first white male mentor, would go on to not only hire me as an adjunct faculty member, but to make me work full-time, and then promote me to Department Director. Under his guidance, I learned how to manage, lead, and administrate not only students, but also a large team of faculty.

I would enjoy this relative peace for a grand total of two years before a major family upheaval: my husband shifted his work focus and decided to return to university to complete his degree. This meant we would be losing all his overtime income, and now needed to find a way to replace that money.

Meanwhile, Steve was resigning from his role to move to another school within the EDMC system—and, in my search, I discovered that a Dean's role was opening up. Hence, we discussed the possibility of my making the move with him and taking on this role. He was only too happy to have me join him on this new adventure. Not so fast, though: enter White Male Mentor #2.

With Steven's resignation, the then-Associate Dean, Ed, had been promoted to Dean, and he needed to fill the role he vacated. That was a very interesting conversation that day:

Ed: So, you know that the Assistant Dean position is open.
Me: Yes.
Ed: Don't you plan to apply?
Me: No.
Ed: Why not?
Me: Because I'm going with Steve to be his new Dean of Student Services at South University.
Ed: Why?
Me: *Sigh*
Ed: But you are who I want to promote.

Me: *Wide-eyed, shocked emoji*

Ed: Okay, can you please apply and consider staying here for the job?

Me: Depends on the pay, and why you want me to apply.

Ed: Okay, we can talk about the pay.

Me: Okay, so why do you want me?

Ed: I can tell you, but it's not politically correct.

Me: *Eyeroll* Go ahead. I asked, didn't I? I'm not easily offended.

Ed: Well, for too many years, it's been three white guys running things. We need to add some change and diversity so that the students have someone they can identify with. You are black and female. The female students need someone they can talk to; they won't talk to a man the way they will to a woman. Plus, as a woman, you have the "mommy" factor, which does help. You can say and do things that I, as a man, cannot in some situations.

Me: *Thinking emoji*

I learned some interesting things that day: first and foremost, Ed wanted me for the job because he thought I was qualified and would do a good job; second, he told me he knew I had the respect of the other team members; third, he thought it would be a good idea to have a woman of color in a position of leadership. He stated that the organization lacked balance—both in terms of gender and race. Ed forever lives in my mind as a leader who was actively working toward helping me achieve BossLadyShip. He continues to be one of my favorite people; this is largely due to the fact that, for the next three years, he would coach me—sometimes with great exasperation—into the role I ultimately wanted: Chief Academic Officer/Vice President of a College.

In all honesty, I was gobsmacked that he had the courage to be as honest with me as he was; however, after working with him for the next three years, I saw that this was exactly who Ed was: honest and straightforward to a fault. I couldn't believe that he'd been brave enough to do the politically incorrect thing and just tell me why, amongst all the persons interviewing, I was who he considered to be the best choice.

We had many days of negotiation, and I did eventually cave and take on additional roles to get to the pay I wanted. We'll discuss negotiation later in this book; it really is a critical skill for women (especially women of color) to learn. I started the job on at least $10,000 less than I should have, and I was fulfilling two roles at the time: I continued to be the Director of a division, as well as a Dean. They were happy to tell everyone that I was the first to do it—and successfully, at that—, but that was not really a feather in my cap; it was me compromising and accepting what I thought I had to in order to accomplish my end goal. Today, I'd tell any mentee of mine to fight harder.

But what's the lesson that needs to be learned at this juncture? I've told this story to women who were outraged that I'd allowed myself to be used as a pawn in the organization. I smile at this, because if I'm a willing participant, then I'm not being used. I learned more in those three years than most people learn in 10. I was fully cognizant that Ed needed me to be good and successful in my role; he had hired me, after all, because I was a woman, and, more importantly, because I was a woman of color—and not just to make a quota, but because he knew I was capable and could be effective in the role. He then spent three years conditioning me to become even more successful. The lesson, therefore, is this: never look a gift horse in the mouth. Sometimes, the success may not come in the package you expect; your job, rather, is to look beyond the package and instead see the opportunities that are ahead of you, and then take advantage of those opportunities when they present themselves.

I looked at the role that both of those men played in my tenure at the Art Institute and credit both of them with the leader I would become. I never realized I was being mentored; quite frankly, I just found them annoying, as they gave me special assignments, talked endlessly to me, and just frustrated my world without end. With hindsight, however, I can easily see that all the while, they were teaching me patience, the skill of honing my emotional intelligence skills, and how to manage, lead, coach, and mentor—without ever once saying that that was what they were doing. They would give me projects and tasks to complete because they wanted me to expand and learn to do more. They would always make time to sit in my office for idle chit-chat and check in with me personally. In Chapter 4, I will elaborate more on how their mentorship helped me to grow as a leader, but it was my experience with these two men which led me to my assumption that I was successful in my leadership journey because of the race and gender of my mentors.

At the end of my research and the collation of the statistics, I found that neither the race nor the gender of the mentor had anything to do with the leadership roles attained by myself or by the group of women who were part of my study; rather, the data indicated that the education, experience, and industry at play were the key factors. So, my master's degree, more than 10 years of experience, and the fact that I worked in education, had been the reasons for my leadership attainment. This allowed me a greater ability to rise and be successful in the field. It would be interesting to see if women in finance or other fields would have dissimilar results!

Now, Chapter 5 of every dissertation asks you to discuss what further plans you have for the dissertation topic. Dissertations are very narrowly defined questions, and, usually, once that question is answered, it begs another; in fact, you're *supposed* to pose the question so that another academician can pursue that avenue—or you can pursue further research.

Upon completing my dissertation, my goal in 2015 was simply to be done and to move on. I was now part of the 1%: I was already a VP, and had taken a few years out of my life to take on this academic pursuit—and now, I could reap the personal satisfaction of saying I'd done it. I had zero plans to take it any further. I remember, during my defense, making platitudes and discussing that I would find conferences to present my findings, knowing full well I planned on doing diddly squat; now, the irony lies in the fact that, five years later, here I am, writing a book which essentially begins where my dissertation ends.

ASSIGNMENT

THIS CHAPTER HAS ESSENTIALLY been about my journey, as well as how I got to a place where I was even qualified to write this book. Now, I want you to take a little trip down memory lane and do something similar for yourself. This is not going to be a rigid process, but I *do* want you to think about all the things that make you unique and special—and then to spend some time just paying homage to yourself and appreciating your journey thus far.

My name is ———————and I was born in ———————.
My cultural background is ———————————
The things I love about my culture are...

———————————————————————
———————————————————————
———————————————————————
———————————————————————
———————————————————————

Because of my culture, I have been given...

———————————————————————
———————————————————————
———————————————————————

_____

_____

The things that are special about me are...

_____

_____

_____

_____

_____

The things I love most about myself are...

_____

_____

_____

_____

_____

Today, as I read this book, my goal is to...

_____

_____

_____

_____

_____

Today, as I read this book, I am grateful for...

_____

_____

_____

_____

_____

Things I've realized as I've been reading that I have never thought of before are...

_____

_____

_____

_____

_____

Great! There's nothing wrong with a little self-love and self-appreciation. You need to be happy with who you are right now and where you are in your journey. The next few chapters will be challenging and ask you to dig deep and do some work, so be happy and proud of yourself as you are right now!

CHAPTER 3:
THE PROFESSIONAL
SELF-AUDIT

Instructions: Now is a good time to grab a notebook and pen that you will use for the remainder of this book. Take notes and jot down important things to come back and reference later. Feel free to also take notes in this book, since it can serve as a workbook for you, too.

SO, HERE'S THE THING: the best place to start is always the beginning, and the first thing you need to do is determine both your personal and professional worth. In completing these two audits, you will then determine the value that you have to yourself, your organization, and your business (if you are self-employed). There are a number of things that go into your audit; some of them are on your resume, and the rest are your life experience. So, grab a pen, and let's start.

A professional self-audit is something that you should do each year. Some people wait until they are looking for a job to work on their resumes, but a professional audit allows you to focus on the new skills and knowledge you've gained each year, add these to your resume and profiles, determine what's missing, and create a plan to fill the missing parts. There are a variety of articles and books on the topic, so, today, we are going to narrow this down to five simple steps.

Step One: Skills Analysis

List all of your skills and break those down into three areas:
  a) Behavioral skills;
  b) Broad-based functional skills;
  c) Job-specific technical skills.

Many people do not spend enough time working through these areas, as they seem like fillers on the resume beneath the job title. However, it's these things that help you to fully appreciate your own skillset, and for others to, too. Let's look at the behavioral or soft skills; what does that really mean? What do those skills look like, and what are the skills that will be needed for the task or the job you need to undertake? Below is a list of behavioral skills that should be focused on, if these are skills you have:

- **Strong Active Listening Skills**. This is the ability to listen to others without forming an opinion while they are talking. This allows you, as a leader, to hear where all parties are coming from in order to make an informed decision.
- **Strong Communication Skills**. This is an often-overlooked skill. Communication involves Party A encoding a message and Party B decoding the message

that Party A meant to convey. Often, conflict occurs because communication did not occur as a result of the encoded message not matching the decoded message. Hence, strong, effective communication skills are an asset.

- **Empathy**. While some see this as a "bleeding heart", it's actually the ability to see things from another's perspective, and this is *critical* for a leader. You cannot be an effective leader if you don't understand where others are coming from. This is why women of color are in a unique position to understand those who feel unheard and unrepresented. Being empathetic allows a leader to see a different perspective and then factor that into their decision-making.

- **Strong Interpersonal Skills.** You cannot make yourself a leader; instead, it's followers who make you a leader—and people only follow those who they like and respect! Thus, you need strong interpersonal skills and to be likable in order for that to occur.

The next step is to take each of these items and put an example of a time when you've done this successfully. See why you needed the notebook and pen now?

Skillset Name	Times I Used This Successfully to Benefit the Organization
Listening	
Communication	
Empathy	
Interpersonal	

While these notes won't be on your resume, they create the blueprint for future conversations that you'll undoubtedly have. Our male counterparts are quite good at tooting their own horns; they have no problem with telling everyone and anyone about their successes. Women, on the other hand, are less likely to brag; it's not seen as "ladylike". In line with this, women of color are even less likely to do so, since we are simply doing the work that needs to be done. With this in mind, we need to disabuse ourselves of the notion that people being aware of the benefits we bring to the table somehow makes us less feminine.

Instead of being modest about your accomplishments, you need to catalog them carefully with details and results. At the end of each year (or during your routine evaluation period), document these as accomplishments so that both you and the leadership team are aware of the strengths and achievements you bring to the table! Notably, you should be discussing on a quarterly basis evaluations of the projects you are working on. Oftentimes, you're only as good as your most recent project, so make sure that your accomplishments are kept upfront and visible. Further, if, for any reason, you are moving to a new organization, you'll have a detailed accounting of the project and the steps you used to accomplish your tasks in this way. Many employers enjoy seeing how you think and operate, and having these details will assist in that.

Being able to clearly state your strengths and how they benefit the organization will allow you to negotiate for raises, promotions, and other benefits; further, ensuring that you are fully cognizant of your skills will lessen the blight of imposter syndrome that often plagues women.

A lot has been discussed about women and imposter syndrome, and I will be honest: I never heard of this term until a few years ago. Clearly, I was living under a rock! The term refers to a collection of feelings where women feel inadequate despite being successful, as they suffer from self-doubt and feeling like they don't have the right intellect and/or experience to justify the success they have achieved, despite there being an abundance of proof to the contrary.

The first time someone asked me how I overcame this, I was a tad flummoxed: I'm Jamaican, and the notion that I wasn't qualified or didn't deserve the roles I'd had had never occurred to me. Remember, matriarchal society! So, rather than thinking on how I overcame this, I instead concentrated on why I had never had it in the first place. I then established guidelines on how to ensure that any women that I mentored quickly moved past this stumbling block.

Looking back, I lived in Jamaica until I was 19 years old, during which time my mother was a Vice President and my father a CEO. I was raised in a home with a woman who was in charge. I never saw her question or second-guess herself, and my father was proud that his wife was bright and, quite frankly, expected me, his daughter, to follow suit—and he certainly never second-guessed her, either! His nickname for my mom was Management, and mine was Administration—which attributed to why I never experienced imposter syndrome. My entire upbringing was predicated by the fact that I was capable, and competent, and would be given a title that reflected this. I assumed that I was going to go to college, work hard, and eventually get a business card with my name on a door. The day my name *was* on the door, I took a picture, because my life was exactly on target. I was 23.

However, imposter syndrome is real, and I see it every day in the women I work with: they're more than happy to share their ideas, ire, and dreams with me, but when the time comes for them to share it with the brass or the decision-makers, they're mute; they downplay their knowledge and skills by using language such as, "Well I may not be right or have all the information, but...", "I don't want to ruffle any feathers...", "Maybe we should just do this, if it's easier for you...", and, "I'm not the one in charge...".

Instead of standing firm in the knowledge that they *do* know, that they are experts, that their points are valid, and that they have earned the right to hold the jobs they have and do the work they do, they deliberately sabotage themselves because they somehow don't believe they're worthy or valid. Remember, you (and *only* you) can determine your value and worth; and then it's up to you to demonstrate that value and worth to whoever it needs to be demonstrated to.

Over the years, as I've mentored a variety of women, I've found some strategies that assist me in moving women past these feelings of inadequacy. As a leader, these are useful strategies for you to employ, and, if you find yourself struggling with these issues, then simply find an accountability partner you trust and begin to work through these strategies one at a time.

Your value cannot be set by others. It is determined through knowing your own self worth. Know your worth. Then establish your value. Both are non-negotiable!

Strategies to Overcome Imposter Syndrome

- **Discussing their education and skills and what they are bringing to the table.**

- **Asking them about their short-, mid-, and long-term goals and plans they have for getting there.** This is often very difficult for women, as they have not thought this through. I like to have lunch and talk about this and give them homework to do, and then we discuss it a week later;.

- **Discussing the things they will need to do to get there, as well as any possible roadblocks and how they will overcome such roadblock.** Women of color have very unique cultural and community challenges when attempting to change the script: many times, self-growth and self-improvement is seen as either rejection of cultural or core values, or them attempting to be white. Not everyone is supportive, and women of color will sometimes need to find a new tribe of like-minded women who'll support them on their journey to facilitate them doing this. The great thing about the current environment is that there are a plethora of groups, organizations, conferences, and meetups which allow women of color to find women they can share experiences with, as well as network with.

- **Determining what training they will need to help them accomplish their goals.** As a mentor, I often have the opportunity to see the strengths and areas of growth opportunity in my mentees, so it's easy for me to simply state where they can best benefit from training. If, however, you do not have a mentee, then simply have regular discussions with your supervisor about areas s/he believes would help you be better in your current role or prepare you for future roles in the organization;.

- **Discussing what they learned after each training and how they will implement these tools moving forward.** If you're going to do all this work, it's important to put it into play immediately.
- **Having regular, routine check-ins to ensure they are staying on-target.** I've become an accountability manager for them.
- **Completing projects** that they can:
  a) do successfully because of current skillset;
  b) take on, but requires them to work harder by doing things outside their comfort zone.
- **Presenting their ideas and project accomplishments** either via email or in a meeting so that they can take both accountability and kudos for projects.

I set the ball rolling for mentees, but at the end of the day, it'll be up to each woman to determine her own self-worth so that she can value herself—and, in this way, others will value her, too.

If you haven't already started, let's get cracking on that behavior audit skillset analysis.

Overcoming Imposter Syndrome On Your Own

The hardest thing for you will probably be admitting that you have feelings of self-doubt about your own skills and abilities, either because of your own internal monologue, or because you are being impacted by the thoughts, actions, and words of others. Regardless, the first step in fixing a problem is actually admitting that the issue exists; there's no shame if this is how you're currently feeling! You just need to decide that this is a temporary situation, and that while you're here now, there's no need to take out a mortgage on this address; you could, in fact, choose to break the lease and move to a nicer address!

As part of my research to write this book, I did a lot of Googling, and found two very interesting articles: one was published in *Marie Claire* in 2016, where both Jennifer Lopez and Meryl Streep admitted to feelings of imposter syndrome. So, don't for a *minute* feel that this is relegated to just you; many very successful people sometimes feel this way.

You think, "Why would anyone want to see me again in a movie? And I don't know how to act anyway, so why am I doing this?"
> —Meryl Streep (*Marie Claire*, November 11, 2016)

Even though I had sold seventy million albums, there I was feeling, like, "I'm no good at this."
> —Jennifer Lopez (*Marie Claire*, November 11, 2016)

I read another article from 2017, published in *The Cut*, in which some 25 women talked about their feelings on imposter syndrome and self-doubt. Amongst those who were women of color were Lupita Nong'o, Penelope Cruz, Mindy Kaling, Tracee Ellis Ross, and Padma Lakshmi. These are all women in the public eye who are viewed as beautiful, talented, accomplished, and successful—yet they, too, were plagued with these feelings. However, what is important for us to focus on is not that they *experienced* these feelings, but rather that they worked to *overcome* these feelings and continue on to achieving and accomplishing. It is human and natural to feel some level of fear, anticipation, and stress; however, the important thing is to do some serious self-talk and use strategies to move yourself to a new reality. This is all with the objective of allowing you to accomplish the goals and tasks that you've set for yourself.

Unfortunately, the world is not set up so that women of color have immediate role models of success, although it's now much better than it has been in years past. Indeed, while seeing black and Hispanic/Latina women in the media is becoming increasingly common, Asian and Indian women of color still have much less representation of themselves in the media or in business to be able to serve as a yardstick. As such, these women of color will likely rely on family to provide them with images of success to help them to overcome feelings of imposter syndrome and self-doubt. The conundrum, however, less in whether it is, in fact, the family who are the ones creating the feelings of self-doubt in the first place.

Sometimes it is the lack of support from family and friends that keeps one down and not so much people outside those circles.
—Lourdes, Miami

Here are some steps to overcoming imposter syndrome if you have no mentor to assist you:

1. **Admit how you're feeling.**
2. **Get a journal and begin to write down when you started to feel this way, and what precipitated this feeling**, whether...
   a) something you're feeling;
   b) something you don't know/understand;
   c) fear of failure or success;
   d) something someone said.

Over the course of a few weeks, you may begin to see a pattern forming as to when you have these feelings of inadequacy...

   a) If it's because of an overall feeling, then creating a powerful vision board and using affirmations will help you overcome this.
   b) If it's something that you don't understand, then embark upon a plan to educate yourself and learn about it.

c) If you have a fear of success or failure, then focus on your vision board and affirmations to help you overcome those feelings.

d) If it's someone or a group of someone's who are derailing your move to personal growth and success, then you have two choices:

    i.   I advocate talking so that you can bring to their attention how their words and actions make you feel. If that doesn't work, then:

    ii.   You will need to find a way to minimize your interaction with those who create an area of negativity which does not allow you to continue on your growth journey.

Create a vision board creating the person you want to be. Use powerful words when creating this new world for yourself. I've included images of my own #2020VisionBoards (yes, I had two; my dreams for my life were too big for just one!).

3. **Find a mentor.** A mentor can be a huge asset in helping you overcome your personal unproductive internal monologues, helping you to learn and grow as well as being an accountability partner for you.

4. **Find your tribe!** The idea of #WomenSupportingWomen is a key component to helping women build self-confidence and self-esteem. Being around like-minded women who are all about being #BossLadies will help you to keep your goals in mind and not lose track of yourself or the legacy you're in the processs of building.

Functional Skills

Here is where you begin to focus on the hard skills you have. I often find that functional skills and some behavioral skills do have some overlap, so don't stress if you find that functional skills fall into this area! Functional skills are broader than technical skills; while functional leadership skills apply to a wide cross-section of jobs and settings, technical skills are specific to a given job or task.

Below is a list of transferrable functional skills required for every #BossLadyLeader, regardless of color or culture.

Negotiation	Mediation	Managing Remote Groups
Multi-Tasking	Creative Problem-Solving	Public Speaking
Collaboration	Motivation	Building Self-Esteem
Team-Building	Time Management	Conflict Resolution
Creativity	Active Listening	Oral and Written Communication

Just as you did with the behavioral skills, you should now sit down and put an example beside each of these items in order to clearly know where your skills are, as well as how you can be an asset to an organization. As a hiring manager, I often use behavior-based questions so as to determine the way in which a potential employee will handle any given situation. Hence, if you have examples to illustrate how you managed these areas in your various roles, it will make it easy for you to answer questions when asked—not to mention the fact that employers will be impressed that you clearly understand how specific skills work in a wide variety of scenarios!

- **Negotiation**. This is a skill which few women possess and women of color lag even further behind in. In an attempt to climb the corporate ladder, women have often accepted the terms that were given to them by men with regard to pay and benefits, and, as a result, women today continue to make less than their male counterparts, women of color meanwhile making even less than their white female counterparts. Remember, I discussed my own experience with pay disparity. This is what has propelled women into the field of business ownership in such large numbers: indeed, the National Association of Women Business Owners states that there are 11.6 million firms owned by women in the United States, employing more than 9 million people and generating 1.7 trillion in sales. Furthermore, companies owned by women account for 39% of privately held organizations, and contribute 8% of employment and 4% of revenue. Of these 11.6 million firms, 5.4 million are owned by women of color, accounting for the employment of 2.1 million people and generating $361 billion in revenue annually. Women wanted—and *still* want—the ability to have greater control over their earning potential. Learning how to negotiate for one's own monetary worth is of key importance, and, so as to continue this chain, teaching other women to do the same is the next most important factor. It is critical that women of color are seeking ways to empower other women of color once they learn the rules of success: each one passing on the lessons they have learned to another will ensure that the success message and tools continue to be translated and taught to others, and then the next generation. Once women of color learn this skill for themselves, they'll then be in a position to employ it across a number of platforms (e.g., learning how to negotiate with buyers, sellers, and vendors to get better prices and terms). As a minority business, there are several advantages that women—and especially women of color—can leverage to their benefit, and, on the internal front, interpersonal negotiation is also important with employees and team members with regard to projects, deadlines, and accountability. Indeed, it is often better to negotiate to a good outcome than to lay down a dictate that is then ignored.

- **Conflict Resolution and Mediation.** These two items go hand-in-hand. The one thing that is sure to occur is conflict, but it's important to learn that conflict is not always a bad thing; sometimes, it can serve to highlight an underlying issue that needs to be addressed. Conflict occurs when there is a violation of expectations on the part of an individual or a group, and in order for good relations to be restored and everyone to return to the status quo of an efficient and effective operation, leaders will need to mediate through the conflict. Considering there are entire books and courses written on this issue, I won't spend too much time discussing it here, but it's still essential to note that BossLadyLeaders must know how to effectively diffuse a volatile situation and then bring everyone to the table, listen carefully to all sides, and help move all parties to a resolution. For years, women were thought to be better at this task than men because we are natural mothers and socialized to be collaborative and solution-oriented—and this doesn't seem to be far from the truth. Regardless, the ability to do this is an important skill, so don't allow any sexist notions to prevent you from learning and honing this skill. Indeed, while women of color are unfortunately seen as "less threatening" most of the time (and while such an assumption can be frustrating), it does give us a certain ability to go into a situation and diffuse it, as no one believes we are there to make anyone else uncomfortable. At the end of the day, it's a win for the organization, and a personal win for you in your list of achievements.

- **Managing Remote Groups.** In today's global economy, many organizations hire people who do not live in the same geographical area, and those groups are expected to be as cohesive as ones working in the same building. Hence, the ability to organize across multiple geographic areas and time zones is an asset to any organization.

- **Time Management and Multitasking.** Few leaders have the luxury of being able to sit down and focus on a single thing for weeks on end. Often, project completion requires managing multiple smaller projects, so time management naturally becomes a critical asset and skill in managing multiple projects, groups, and people. I, personally, am a list-maker, and I enjoy going into the office each day and making lists of things to accomplish and then marking them off at the end of the day. I tried using a Franklin Covey planner, but I found that it never worked well for me; I just loved my lists! However, in the last year, I started using a calendar to keep track of projects, and this year, I've embarked upon using a series of planners (personal, projects, gratitude). Next year, I'll be able to report how successful that endeavor was. Indeed, I was amazed at the amount of women who are part of the planner community, and, as I looked at ways to use planners, I realized that several women of color have carved a space for themselves in the planner community with planners, stickers, and accessories for women of color. This is a great example of women of color looking at an industry and not finding themselves represented, so creating products for women like themselves. This is also a great lead-in to problem-solving.

- **Creative Problem-Solving.** Problems will occur; however, it is the way in which you take all your skills to solve issues that is critical, as this is what will keep the organization functioning at optimal capacity. It is also something that all leaders must have the ability to do. Take note of the word "creative", something that has become somewhat of a cliché term in today's business environment. Your goal here is to use your personal skills and abilities to find solutions to issues that others might not have thought of; to solve the issue at hand and do the following:
  - o Achieve the goals;
  - o Allow everyone to have a small win so that no one person or group reaps all the benefits;
  - o See how "thinking outside the box" can help to create new ways to do things that align with the organizational goals and/or the goals that you have created for your organization.

Example: I recently encountered an artist who created unusual pieces of art. She had about 10 pieces she wanted to sell, and was struggling because she wanted to price each piece at $125-$150, but couldn't get people to pay more than $50 for each piece. She was becoming exceedingly despondent, and was thinking about giving up her art altogether. I looked at the pieces and was reminded of the abstract art I'd often seen in hotels. Thus, I suggested that she should take the pieces and do the following:

a. find out how much it would cost to make prints of each in a variety of sizes;

b. Contact hotels, motels, and B&Bs and see if any of them were looking for pieces for their locations.

I explained to her that if she were to say find a location that had even 50 rooms and was renovating, they would need two prints per room. She could charge $25-$50 for each print (and she'd still retain the original piece), and make $2,500-$5,000. She had been thinking of her art as an individual sale, rather than looking at the commercial options. Problem-solving often requires that for you to remove the emotion and attachment to the issue so that it can be viewed dispassionately.

- **Public Speaking**. Some leaders are natural public speakers in front of a group; others have to learn the skill. Regardless of which category you fall in, the bottom line is that all leaders *must* have the ability to speak to their teams and convey their thoughts, feelings, and expectations in a way that is inspirational, uplifting, motivating, and holding the team and its members accountable to results. If you are not comfortable with speaking to groups, then I suggest joining organizations where you get practice; after all, as a manager, you address groups, and as a business owner, you must be comfortable talking about and selling yourself, your business, and your ideas.

- **Collaboration**. As a teacher, I never thought it was a good idea to give tests that required students to simply regurgitate information; what I needed to know was if the students understood the concept and could translate and apply it. Hence, in my classroom, I was all about collaboration and sharing, and was interested in ensuring that students could also help one another with their concepts. After all, if you can teach something to someone else, that means you truly understand the concepts. This also applies to the workplace: the goal of a leader is to encourage ongoing collaboration, not only within a team, but also across teams and across departments. Doing this will mean that everyone understands the value of each person on the team and in the organization, and that you, the leader, are actively working to promote this. As an entrepreneur, you'll always be seeking ways to collaborate with other businesses: collaboration increases your reach and the potential to get more clients and, thus, sales and revenue.

- **Motivation**. There are entire schools of thought around what motivates employees, and, as a leader, you should be well-versed on all of these schools of thought. You should be able to discuss the various types of motivation; after all, you'll need to employ all at some point in your leadership tenure in order to meet all the organizational goals. The most important note to remember, however, is that motivation is ʰividual, and, as a leader, it is critical that you rstand what motivates each member of the team individually, not as a group. As an entrepreneur, you're looking at motivation from two points: first, what is going to motivate the buyer to want your product; and second, what the motivation of your team/staff to help you get to my business goal. What does achieving the business goal do for your team? What's in it for them? It is critical that your employees and team are not just doing what they do for a check—and, to avoid this, you need to take it upon yourself to understand the personal motivation of your staff: if you can positively feed what motivates them, that creates a motivated, happy individual and, thus, team.

- **Building Self-Esteem.** Considering, as a woman of color, you'll be working with other women in the midst of imposter syndrome, you'll need to develop a strategy to help these women to realize their own potential and grow into being the best person they can be. Of course, you'll also need to build the self-esteem of anyone on your team or within your realm of influence. It's very important that you learn how to pay it forward and to build others up!

- **Team-Building**. You're only a leader because there's a team you're leading, and, as such, you're constantly working on team dynamics. There are many different kinds of teams, and your goal is to lead a high-performance team; however, this can only be the case with constant building maintenance. Learning the dynamics of teams, as well as how to build a dynamic, high-performance team, is another key leadership requirement. As a woman of color, it is essential that you understand that you may come across resentment from men who don't believe you have the ability to lead the team effectively—because you're a woman and because you're a woman of color. However, as long as you walk in with an awareness of the possible issues, you can then manage the situation accordingly. This is where your strong interpersonal skills will become necessary: it'll be up to you to ensure that you are a good blend of likable and knowledgeable so that they develop a respect for your ability enough to be held accountable to your expectations. Is it all a game? Yes, it is, and your job is to learn to play the game well— and win!

- **Creativity.** There is always more than one way to skin a cat. Often, we get stuck in a rut of doing the same things we've always done, in turn failing to realize that there might be a new, better, more effective ways to do things. Embracing the new is what I classify as being creative. As a teacher, I've always been a fan of rewarding our faculty in ways they like. For years, I would buy items, package them, and send them out— and then came Amazon and the ability to send an e-gift card! This was simply the best thing since sliced bread: instead of forcing my team to enjoy what I gave them, they now had the entire Amazon store at their fingertips, as well as the money to make a desired purchase! I thought I was being pretty creative here.

- **Effective Oral and Written Communication.** I cannot express enough how important these two skills are. Under behavioral skills, we discussed that what makes effective communication is the ability to ensure that the message you mean to give is the one that is actually received. Accordingly, it's a good idea, as a leader, to carefully plan all communications very carefully: start by considering what you want the message to be; then take the audience into consideration; then factor in the goal you wish to achieve. Take these three things and craft either a verbal or written message geared toward achieving these things, ensuring to keep it short, simple, informational, motivational, and inspiring. Always remember to include yourself in the message so that they understand that this is a "we" and not a "you" initiative.

Technical Skills

This is fairly self-explanatory: take the specific job skills that you have that relate to your job, and create a list of those. If you're a computer programmer, list the specific programs you work with and the certifications that you have; if you're a marketing specialist, list the various types of marketing and project software you work with and the marketing campaigns you're able to manage; if you're an educator, list the education credentials you have, the various levels and ages you've taught, and the special skills that you have (e.g., online education; Google platforms).

Step Two: Polishing the Crystal Ball

My son is currently 17 years old. He'll go to college in 2021 and graduate with his first degree (hopefully!) in 2025. That's five years from now, and you know what? In all likelihood, the world will have created jobs that don't currently exist, and he could or may need new skills to do that job in order to be effective. Few of us know what the future holds, but a good self-audit involves keeping abreast of industry and societal trends and determining if and how those skills will impact your job.

Back in 2008, when all of us were logging onto Facebook to find our friends, none of us really understood that 12 years later, social media would be the marketing juggernaut that it currently is. Companies now have entire departments dedicated to monitoring their social media and figuring out who the influencers are who can best help their business. Let's face it: being a social media influencer is a legitimate job. Who knew that this would even ever be a thing? Now, there are entire courses, forums, and training platforms set up to understand social media platform algorithms so that businesses can be successful in the medium—and my mentor is, in fact, a social media coach.

One of the jobs that is hot and current in 2020 is being a virtual assistant. Many entrepreneurs need someone to assist them with any number of tasks, from keeping their calendar, to responding to emails and providing customer support—and sometimes, this is needed because they have a full-time job, or because they are a one-woman show and simply don't have sufficient time to do all the tasks or the capital to hire an experienced administrative staff member. So—*et voila*—, the advent of the virtual assistant: someone who may or may not be in the same geographical area, but manages the administrative tasks you need, often inclusive of social media. 10 years ago, before the advent (and explosion!) of smartphones, apps, and virtual office software, the notion of being a virtual assistant was not a position many would have given much thought to; and yet now, a single person can have four or five clients, each paying them $800-$2,000/month, depending on the tasks.

Part of your audit involves ensuring that you keep yourself informed in terms of shifts in politics, social issues, social reforms, climate and environmental concerns, and any number of things that may shift how you will be successful in your role. When I first began doing presentations on generational training back in 2014, the field of diversity and inclusion was not a very large one; and today, in the #MeToo, #BlackLivesMatter, and #NeverGain era, the landscape for diversity and inclusion training has broadened exponentially. I've been fortunate enough to have spoken and written about the need to understand generational and cultural differences in order to have a harmonious organization; one organization even asked me to discuss this topic as part of their cultural enhancement initiative.

It's imperative that you keep yourself current, relevant, and educated on all the items that will impact the organization you work for (or the business you're creating and/or growing). There are a number of ways to do this:

1. **Subscribe to a couple of news sources.** The economic and political climate can impact your ability to import or export items or receive the raw materials you will need for your company.

2. **Read as much as you can (e.g., books, articles, blogs).** She who has information is the #BossQueen, and you need to have all the information that'll help make solid business decisions.

3. **Join forums.** You do not exist in a vacuum! There are others out there who you can learn from, share with, and collaborate with.

4. **Attend meetups.** While we live in a digital age, there is still something to be said about a face-to-face meeting. This also allows you to forge new personal, social, and business connections. The world still operates on the principle that "it's not what you know, it's who you know".

5. **Network.** Even I admit that I don't do enough of this for my own company. This is critical: every #BossLadyLeader should be attending at least one professional networking event each month. This keeps you out there in the industry and knowing who all the players are. More importantly, they know who *you* are!

5. **Attend conferences.** This is a great way to get in education and networking in one swoop—and, if you like to travel, hopefully the conference is in a city you don't know and can explore. It's also an opportunity for you to make new contacts in an area that is not your base location.

This is where you can take a pause from reading, pick up your phone, and begin surfing. Look for the above items and subscribe to those news sources, forums, and meetup groups. Jot these down in your notebook (or on this page, if it's easier!), or bookmark them in your phone; then, make a note of the conferences that would be beneficial for you to attend.

A recent article in *Inc Magazine* by Sonia Thompson (dated 08/22/2019) made me exceedingly sad: while it lauded black women as being the most educated, they were lagging behind with pay equity. According to the Institute for Women's Policy Research, black women earn 61 cents to the dollar for the same job done by men. Even more shocking is the estimation that black women will not earn those 39 cents until 2119, while white women will bridge that gap by 2055. This is what has triggered black women to flee the corporate world in pursuit of becoming entrepreneurs. Ms. Thompson lists three key areas to improve this trend:

  a. Focus on achieving pay equity;
  b. Mentorship and networking;
  c. Access to capital and resources.

Earlier, I shared one story of pay inequity; now, I will share another. There are schools of thought on whether or not we should share how much money we make. This is in light of the fact that traditional corporations like to keep pay a taboo subject, since there is no pay equity: white men continue to get paid the most, followed by other men, then white women, then women of color. Of course, this means that publicizing pay is *not* a good idea. It would create huge levels of discontent within the team; I can confirm this personally! I know what it's like to be a senior staff member with more education and tenure—only to find myself making some $30,000 less than a white male counterpart. Ordinarily, I would not have known of this disparity (I actually found out by accident), but that inequity stuck in my craw. I would eventually discuss the matter with both HR and my boss, and the situation was remedied. Before this, however, they tried to explain that people in some departments made more than others. I won't lie, I was quite happy for the sizeable increase, and decided to live with the factors that led to the inequity: quite frankly, I wasn't in a position to do anything else. As women—especially women of color—, we often see inequity and find there to be not much we can do about it except to create a new reality for ourselves—hence why millions of women of color have abandoned the corporate life to be entrepreneurs!

Let me now segue back to ensuring that you are ready to take on the challenges you choose. If you do a professional self-audit each year, you'll begin to notice when new skills and education are required for either a) the role you currently have, b) the role you wish to pursue, or c) the business you wish to begin or grow. What you will need to do to close that gap between your current skills and knowledge?

What's going to be needed will be discussed in the next point. It's just very important that you understand the need to always do a temperature check to ensure you don't fall too far behind.

I hold employment in the field of education, and about four or five years ago, the industry shifted: in the 1970s, there was a trend toward skills-based training and apprenticeships, the history of people of color being that these were jobs which we held. People of color were almost always tradespeople. However, the 1980s and 1990s saw a distinct shift toward formal education, and people of color, especially women, began earning college degrees. Today, women of color far outstrip their male counterparts with degrees and advanced degrees. Degrees were previously seen as the entre into the corporate world, and organizations used this as part of the vetting process. This means that there are a vast number of highly qualified and experienced women of color in the workplace, and, accordingly, we need to ensure that we are part of the decision-making processes within organizations.

As degrees became more and more expensive and millennials accrued some $350 billion in debt, the trend toward education began to shift back to training and skills acquisition. Hence, the question most employers today ask is, "Do you have the skills and experience we need?" If that is a yes, then organizations will hire without the degree. Further, when Google and Amazon came out and said they no longer required degrees in 2019, this well and truly shook up the education industry—but, as someone doing a professional audit, your job is to look at who is hiring and what the skills and experience are that they are looking for. If what they're looking for and what you have do not match, then you have one task: fill the gap.

Step Three: Filling the Gap with Education and Training

About a year ago, someone suggested that we, as a school, should create a social media course that teaches people how to use the various platforms. They were pretty pleased with themselves, telling me how much money we could make, but I had to pause and ask them why they thought someone would pay for something that's available for free. They looked at me in consternation. Free? Yes, I told them; free. There is so much training out there on how to use social media platforms that it's borderline mindboggling: not only do

Facebook and Instagram provide training, but many other sources do, too. In fact, some social media influencers/coaches themselves provide free training.

There is a course and a training for almost anything anyone would wish to pursue. Now, there are some God-awful courses out there on the Internet, and I've paid for and taken some. There are many people who use gimmicks to get people to sign up and take a course, and then when they *do*, provide very little information, or a program that is so badly structured that people never finish the course. However, the problem is, of course, that they've already paid for the course. Hence, it's important to vet who is offering the course to determine if this is a course you want to take—and just a word of advice: any course where the original price was $499 and has now been reduced to $49.99 is probably not worth your time. Who discounts their programs by *that* much?

Let's say you decide you want to open an online boutique; you've been scrolling through Facebook and Instagram, and you've been shopping up a storm. You think that if *you're* spending a couple hundred dollars each month online, then maybe this is a great way to make some money and become self-employed. Now, you need to figure out how to do this: there are courses out there on how to set up an online store, so the first thing you should do is sign up to take this course; or maybe you're a HR Manager, and you realize that your talent acquisition skillsets are lagging behind. You've been going to SHRM meetings and realizing that your counterparts are having great success in hiring using specific algorithms in the hiring platforms, or have partnered with organizations offering assessment tools to align talent with open positions.

You recognize the industry is forging forward and that you're still stuck using skills of the past. This is the time for you to sign up for some training seminars and begin reading more about new ideas in HR Management. It's not always necessary to go back to school and Square One to learn new skills or gather new information; sometimes, simply keeping current with industry publications will keep you abreast of changes, and other times, you may need to register for a course—and if this is the case, you'll need to begin investigating where you can find these courses.

My suggestion is to always look for what is offered for free first. What do the major industry platforms offer? Oftentimes, if you're a member of an organization, there's free training offered to its members, so take advantage of those first. Most conferences usually have free training, too, so be sure to take advantage of these before spending resources. However, if you feel that certifications are warranted or that they make you more marketable (both inside and outside of your organization), it might be a good idea to investigate your options and determine a timeframe and cost that are most doable for you.

If you decide to embark upon formal education because you feel it's necessary for growth and advancement, then spend time on sites like Glassdoor, LinkedIn, and Indeed, and examine what skills and levels of education are being sought by employers. If formal education is going to take you years to complete, you run the risk of being out of date even before you've begun. Remember that education often lags behind the marketplace by a time period of year to 18 months, all because of the time it takes to approve new educational programs.

As an educator, I'm a proponent of ongoing education and training, and, while some roles do require formal education, there are many ways for you to become skilled, experienced, and a good option for hire and advancement, *without* expending resources. An education is an important asset, and is certainly one you should seek to acquire; however, putting yourself into excessive debt to get such education and/or training is not a good position to take. Your goal as a leader is to be knowledgeable and skilled *without* the burden of debt.

It's difficult getting capital to begin new entrepreneurial enterprises, and having a large student loan debt burden when you're attempting to secure a business loan may accordingly not necessarily be the best course of action—so be smart about the training and education that you undertake. Research all the the methods there are for you to fund your education. On the flipside, the Small Business Association will look favorably on you if you have undergone some education and training in the areas you're beginning your business. So, the point is: get the training and education necessary for your enterprise; just be smart about it and incur a minimal amount of debt.

Step Four: Create a Gameplan with a Blueprint

Okay, so you've done a self-audit of your skills, you've looked into the crystal ball of the future, and you've determined what you need to fill the gap between your current skills and those you need to move forward. Now, it is time for you to create a blueprint for accomplishing your goals! If at this point you feel a little overwhelmed, that's okay; just breathe and take a minute. All us #LadyBosses get to that point, and, while it seems scary at the time, it's actually a great place to be.

Why is that, you ask? Because it means you've done some serious introspection and come to a lot of truths based on that self-examination; it also means you understand your strengths and the areas you need to improve upon. It means you're actively embracing the actions required for continuous growth and improvement. This is an excellent place to be, but you don't want to reside here too long; you need to think of this as the early stages of gentrification. Your goal is to stay here just long enough to see what you need to see, learn what you need to learn, and earn what you need to earn—and then sell for a profit and move on to an even bigger investment!

Now is the time for you to set about creating a blueprint for your success. First, start by asking and answering the following questions.

In this book, I use the term "leadership"; however, it's important to note that leadership also involves creating or growing your own business. The skills needed to lead a team or start/grow a business are all the same; so, if you're reading this and think it's not speaking directly to you, please note that it does! All these skills I discuss are ones I used to both get to all my leadership roles, as well as to branch out and create my own business.

So, let's begin on the blueprint for success!

1. Am I currently in a leadership role? Am I currently a #BossLady CEO?

_____

_____

_____

_____

_____

2. Which and what type of leadership role am I seeking? What type of business do I want to have?

_____

_____

_____

_____

_____

3. Based on my self-audit and skills assessment, do I have all the skills I need to be a successful leader? If yes, what are they?

_____

_____

_____

_____

_____

4. Where is the gap that I need to fill? What's missing from my business plan?

_____

_____

_____

_____

_____

5. Do I need to take any courses? Undertake special training? Get special licensure?

_____

_____

_____

_____

_____

6. If so, where are these courses located? When do they occur? Is there a cost?

_____

_____

_____

_____

_____

7. Do I need to pursue advanced education? Try to be specific.

_____

_____

_____

_____

_____

8. What are the costs associated with training or formal education?

_____

_____

_____

_____

_____

9. What is the timeframe that I will need to get into my desired leadership role or open my own enterprise?

_____

_____

_____

_____

_____

10. How am I going to fund this? What options are available to me?

_____

_____

_____

_____

_____

The above questions ask if you know how you plan to fund your journey into leadership or entrepreneurship. This is, of course, another area of angst and trepidation for women of color: many white women have options for funding that are simply not available to women of color. Many did not grow up with access to people with money, influence, or affluence— often the components that allow those with access to opportunities not available to others. They do not receive inheritances or bequests which allow them to become financially independent, and women of color are not traditionally from wealthy or upper middleclass families. Hence, starting any business will often mean self-funding or seeking funding from a bank or other sources.

I feel that the issues are as much issues of color as issues of class. The two are very closely related. My business has actually been very well-received in my area, but growth is difficult. We have so far been a self-funded entity, but in order to grow, [we] will have to receive funding from either banks or private investors. I don't come from a background where I know anyone who can help with that, and I feel, whether accurate or not, that banks are less willing to give me a chance.

—Melanie, NC

Many years ago, when I was able to get life insurance, the broker encouraged me to think about making insurance sales my side-gig. He had recruited many women of color into selling insurance, many of which having been teachers who simply didn't make enough to buy homes or afford their children a good education. Selling insurance became their side-hustle, with an important outcome: they would take out small policies, which would gradually increase over the years. What having a life insurance policy did (and does) is create generational wealth: when these moms passed, this allowed their children and grandchildren the same luxuries that non-minorities had been experiencing for years.

Step Five: Making Review a Habit

While Step Five is not in and of itself a new step, it is a necessary step, and there should be time set aside to engage in this process. If you're a new LadyBoss (a.k.a., a BabyBossLady!), then you'll begin this review step later in your personal growth process. You're actively working on building the training, education, and skills you need take you into leadership—a process that can take a few weeks, months, or years, especially if you decide to pursue formal education. However, the important part is that you're actively working toward achieving the goal you outlined in Step Two (Polishing the Crystal Ball). What you will be doing, however, is achieving small goals for yourself and working towards reaching each of those larger goals.

For more experienced LadyLeaders, this habit of reviewing ensures you're staying current and relevant, and that you're doing regular check-ins on those skills and experiences (i.e., you're taking refresher courses, attending conferences, meeting new people at networking events, and keeping yourself informed through your commitment to reading and ongoing training and development). My own Step Five has been writing this book and completing additional courses in life coaching, mindfulness, and female empowerment!

I went looking for pictures from my early jobs and found the previous. This is the phone list from my first job, circa 1993. I had an office number and an extension. I was already a BabyBossLady, and didn't even know it!

CHAPTER 4:
EMOTIONAL INTELLIGENCE
AND BOSSLADYSHIP

I MAY BE AGING myself, but I was in my thirties when I first resonated with the term "emotional intelligence". In my twenties, I'd heard the term "emotional quotient", but that was so far out of my reality (i.e., one just trying to make ends meet) that I didn't pay much attention to it. When I became a manager at 30, however, I found that I now had to become conversant with the term. While it seemed to be fairly self-explanatory to me, I figured I should understand what it actually meant; after all, I knew I'd never be a good manager/leader if I didn't have it. As I looked to become a manager and began reading more management and self-help books, the term kept coming up more and more, and, as a neophyte manager, I knew this was something that if I didn't have, I might need to get quick.

What is emotional intelligence, and why is this important for a BossLady? Well, emotional intelligence is considered to be a necessary skill for any effective leader. Quite simply, emotional intelligence is your ability to be in touch with your own feelings and emotions and, as such, recognize the same emotions in others and have the appropriate action to manage both yours and others' emotions.

The five key components of emotional intelligence are as follows:

- Self-awareness;
- Self-regulation;
- Motivation;
- Empathy;
- Social skills.

Now, let's see if you've been paying attention: do any of the items on this list seem familiar to you? If so, where do you think you've seen them before? If you said in your self-audit, then you get a gold star and move to the front of the line. I'm hoping that you really did take the time to spend some time working through that audit, because now, we're going to see how working through the self-audit will help you to harness your leadership potential to success!

As a minority group, women of color are usually more self-aware, and this is because, sadly, they have to be: minorities are aware of the nuances of things because their success and/or failure often rest in the spaces of these nuances. Women of color are especially attuned to the emotions and feelings of others, as those feelings will likely always impact them. If a member of another group feels that a woman of color has created an issue for them, a woman of color understands that this will become something she'll need to handle, and that it may not turn out in her favor, regardless of whether she's right or wrong. Women of color understand that it is in their best interest if the groups with whom they work or interact do not see them as a threat, combative, or aggressive; hence, they have learned to moderate their behavior in order to be seen as non-threatening and agreeable. This is so that they are able to successfully navigate a professional life with a minimum amount of professional strife.

There is nothing about this reality that is a positive, but nevertheless, it's one that women of color have accepted as a norm. In all fairness, many organizations are now doing a much better job in terms of diversity and inclusion training: organizations understand diversification and globalization, and know that diversity of staff and experience is the lifeblood and strength of an organization. Secondly, many companies wish to avoid unnecessary litigation due to inequitable hiring and cultural organizational norms—and, on the positive side, more women of color are getting into roles where they're seeking to change the corporate cultures they operate in.

However, because of this inequity in the current status quo, women of color have become especially good at understanding the rules of emotional intelligence, since it relates to understanding others' emotions; these are rules they live by on a daily basis. Women of color are constantly measuring the temperature of the culture and environment to determine where there might be landmines that they need to avoid.

There are several advantages to mastering the five rules of emotional intelligence, as follows:

- **It allows women of color to become change agents.**
  The more women of color who are in positions of
  power, the more women of color who can be mentored
  into positions of power. It's when women attain these
  roles that they can begin to change the social structure,
  status quo, and corporate landscape. Lisa Price is the
  owner of Carol's Daughter, and she changed the
  trajectory for women who created companies geared
  toward ethnic groups: when she started her product
  line, there were no such product out there, and so she
  started a revolution which has now boomed as part of
  the "natural hair" market. This, as you're likely already
  aware, allows all women with ethnic or curly hair to
  have a plethora of products they can choose from.
  Now, every celebrity of color, from Tracee Ellis Ross to
  Taraji P Henson, have natural haircare lines. When
  Lisa Price sold her business to L'Oreal, she received a
  lot of backlash, and it took some time before people
  understood that she'd only done what successful
  business people do: you start a business, be the first to
  do it, start a new industry, and then sell it for a huge
  profit, and thus create generational wealth. Lisa Price
  was the quintessential change agent: she understood
  the frustration of women who wanted a natural
  product that worked for them, and then later
  understood her strong position to get a good price for
  selling the company she'd grown for 25 years.

- **It allows women of color to understand their own strengths and weaknesses.** Working through the self-audit would have allowed you to see your areas of vulnerability that you need to work on. At this point, you have an entire education, training, and action plan, so you already have the tools you need to work toward this. You'll always play to your strengths, and you always lead with those. Your areas of vulnerability are things you're always working to improve. You do not run away from them; instead, you embrace them, understanding that this is where you are now, but that it is simultaneously a simple pit stop on your way to where you're working to.

- **It allows women of color to understand that perfection is unattainable and unnecessary.** I've never been a fan of saying that people need to give 100%; as a matter of fact, I've always wondered why it requires death for something to be considered done well! Now, that's not to say you can't put 100% *effort* behind something, but *giving* 100% is just too much, in my opinion—and yes, language and wording is important, because one is about effort, and the other is about dying! With that said, perfection is unattainable—and even if it *were* attainable, last time I checked, the last perfect being walked on water, and the haters still made sure he died. The things that are good about life are life's imperfections. A pearl is the result of an irritation, but we consider it to be perfect;

laughter lines are wrinkles, but they're perfect because they indicate that you know how to experience joy; gray hairs are imperfect, but they're a sign of age, wisdom, and that you've been granted the ability to live another day. Mistakes are inevitable in life, and it's sometimes in those mistakes and errors that we find the solutions to issues that we didn't even know we needed a solution to. Women of color need to know that sometimes, "good" or "great" is okay, because "perfect" is never going to happen. Either that, or redefine what perfection means to you so that it becomes attainable.

- **It allows women of color to understand the importance of balance.** Balance is the act of making sure that everything is in the correct proportion. We operate in multiple pieces, and then just keep adding as we get older: we start life as children, and then we add sibling, cousin, friend, student, employee, life partner, parent, business-owner, and caregiver to that list. At one point in my life, I was balancing at least eight of these 10 items, which would mean I would be giving 12.5% to each of these things—leaving literally nothing for myself! Needless to say, I had two asthma attacks and then fell prey to bronchitis. When you lack balance, the body will figure out a way to help you to recover it. In my case, it forced me to take to my bed, rest, and take the time for myself. My attempt to be all, do all, and be perfect in all areas was clearly unattainable for me. One of the things I usually try to impart when mentoring younger women is that at some point, one thing is more important than the other—and, most importantly, you must constantly fill your own cup. An empty cup cannot give to anything else, after all! Emotional intelligence helps you to determine when each needs to take precedence. At times, being a child to your parent is key; sometimes, we need to help a friend be accountable or be a shoulder or support; and at other times, we need to focus on our children or spouse—and, with all that in balance, we also need to find time to rest, recuperate, and regenerate so that we can rinse and repeat. We spend the first year of our life learning how to balance on two feet, and then the rest of our lives learning that balance is important in *all* things.

- **It allows women of color to appreciate the benefits of curiosity.** Curiosity means that you're always asking questions; you want to know why things happen, as it's what gives you a greater understanding of people, processes, and what outcomes you can expect—and how to manage such outcomes. Curiosity about people is also a good thing: people are different; cultures are different; genders and generations are different. Curiosity means you want to learn more about everything around you because you know how important it is to your personal and professional growth!

- **It allows women of color to understand the importance of practicing praise of others and gratitude for the things they have earned and accomplished.**

NEVER BE A PRISONER OF YOUR PAST.
IT WAS A LIFE LESSON, NOT A LIFE
SENTENCE.

CHAPTER 5:
MENTORSHIP AND
WOMEN OF COLOR

FULL DISCLOSURE: MENTORSHIP IS my thing! The topic of my dissertation that I defended back in 2015 was the mentorship of black women, and, as I discussed at the beginning of this book, I strongly believed that I got to leadership because I was mentored by white men. For five years, I read everything I could about mentorship. I began my in doctorate in 2008 due to my needing a doctoral degree in order to be promoted to being a Dean. Since I worked for a school and the degree would be paid for by the organization, I delved into my studies.

Between 2008 and 2011, I would do all of my coursework and successfully complete my comprehensive exams in the summer of 2011—and, for the following year, I would slowly work on my dissertation and then drop out of the program in 2012. The reason why it was so easy for me to drop out was because I had no accountability partner, and it wasn't until January 2014, when my husband challenged me about being a "quitter", that I decided to return to school: I would finish my research and be ready to conclude the program within a year.

I would defend my dissertation on Martin Luther King Day in 2015. There's a certain irony in my defending on the day in which we celebrate the man whose entire message was about equality! However, the gap in my degree meant that much of the research I'd included in my work in 2011 was no longer appropriate in 2014; the research in your dissertation should not be outside of a five-year window in order for the data to be current—meaning in 2014, I had to find more current data in order to update my dissertation to make it current and relevant.

Does any of this sound similar to things I've discussed before? The need to ensure that you're always staying on top of current events and trends to stay current and relevant? Not only did I learn this as an academician, but I live it as a BossLadyLeader.

I will include some of my findings on mentorship in this chapter, but will attempt to jazz it up a bit; dissertations are generally quite dry and boring! The things I learned, however, become the backbone of my mentorship and leadership styles.

Is Mentorship Important to the Growth of Women of Color?

There is sufficient anecdotal data to support the idea of women of color not having the same opportunities as men (of any race) and non-women of color. My research indicated that women of color would be best served by actively seeking out mentors in their organizations, meaning that women who are opening their own companies and/or growing their companies should also seek out mentors, since these are (and will) be critical to their personal and professional growth. There's a reason that homebuilders use a blueprint: it ensures you know exactly where every brick, nail, wall, and support beam should be for the building to have structural integrity— and, similarly, mentors similarly help to ensure professional success by providing a blueprint to follow.

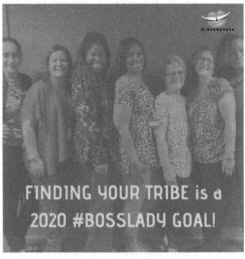

My research also told me that the mantra of #WomenSupportingWomen was not just a hashtag, but was, in fact, a very real thing. Women who are currently in positions of power should actively choose to mentor other women in order to give them the same access which they enjoy—and, on the flipside, women of color need to learn how to make themselves visible so that they can be identified for mentorship. This is the reason why overcoming imposter syndrome is so critical to the success of women of color, and, accordingly, the value of mentorship for women of color lies in helping them to feel better, psychologically and emotionally, as they gain access to enhanced professional and interpersonal growth and skills.

There have even been items delineated for creating successful mentorship programs for women and women of color:

- Mentors are selected based on specific qualifications, including (but not limited to) teaching ability. The ability to listen and employ empathy is also critical.
- Mentors are provided with specific training for their role.
- Mentors are supported in the program through a support and accountability network.
- Mentors are carefully paired with people who they can best help based on personality similarities, and also being within a given age range. Research has found that the best mentorship dyads are with mentors and mentees who are within an eight- to 10-year age range of each other.
- Mentors establish relationships with their mentees based on trust and respect.
- Mentors receive some form of recognition for their work.
- The mentoring program is evaluated and refined on an ongoing basis.

So, if you're a #BossLady in an organization, the above is a framework for supporting women of color in a formalized mentorship program. Organizations should organize mentorship as part of management training, and the managerial review process should include a manager's mentorship ability. Furthermore, managers should be taught how to model and mentor the behaviors that will aid women of color in gaining upward mobility within an organization, and finally, managers should be trained to understand the unique role that mentorship to women will entail.

My research indicated that there are great advantages of women being mentored by other women:

- Female mentors provided greater psychosocial support expressed as personal and emotional guidance.
- Mentees had more opportunities for career advancement when mentored by women than by men (likely due to the visibility they gained as well as supporting their upward mobility).
- Female mentees have a role model whom they use as a model for who and how they need to behave in order to achieve their goals.

Researchers have made the assumption that because women remember how difficult it was for them when they were moving up the corporate ladder, they are generally more willing to help other women with their career development. Women are uniquely aware of the disparity in the workplace, and women of color in particular are even more acutely aware of this, and often attempt to overcompensate in the area of career development due to the abundance of male-dominated professional cultures and organizations.

One of the things that I was always searching for when I was doing my research was the "why": why did women do so much better when aligned with a mentor? My research suggested that men—regardless of race—often see a very clear path to leadership and success, and this is directly as a result of the fact that we live in a male-dominated society. Women, on the other hand, have to figure out how to navigate this path, as there is rarely any structure in place for them to get there.

As women, we use the art of conversation much more than our male counterparts as part of our leadership strategy. Stereotypically, communication is always seen as a strong suit of a woman's management and leadership strategy. Many may see this as sexist, but the leadership tactics used by women are largely because of how we are socialized as little girls: little girls traditionally spend a lot of time playing with other little girls, and so learn the ability to communicate and build teams with other women. In turn, this child's play becomes the building block of #BossLadyLeadership and mentorship tools in the years to come. Women don't always need to be in the spotlight, and are able to showcase the skills and talents of others so that they can be seen and receive accolades, thus leading to advancement. Again, this is why the mantra of "women supporting women" is not just a meme or a hashtag; rather, it's a very real element of helping women become successful leaders and entrepreneurs.

A key component of the communication strategy is the use of storytelling (which feels pretty funny to mention, since that's exactly what I'm doing now: telling stories about my life and those of women I know as I seek to lead women to the same level of leadership I now enjoy!). Women use storytelling as a means to build bridges, create connections, and draw parallels so that those she's trying to influence can see themselves in a new situation with a new reality—namely, one they've designed for themselves.

All the way back in 2003, a study was done that indicated women as often getting into leadership roles due to their ability to pinpoint problems that needed to be solved. In 2018, 15 years later, we saw this in real-time, when a record number of women entered politics after noting the fact that the current political system was broken, thus deciding to step in and fix it. The thing that fascinated me during my ongoing research, however, was a discussion specifically about how black women entered leadership—something that was largely done as a result of the influence of family and church groups. It will be interesting to see how many of you agree with this sentiment!

Women of color constantly live between two worlds: the world of being a woman—a world that 50% of the population occupies—, and the world of their culture—one that is different from the majority and that they thus need to navigate without the help of the majority. Women of color are expected to meet all the traditional requirements of women in society, but then again, they are also expected to represent the community to which they belong. Here, you can see that, in essence, they aren't allowed to be individuals; instead, they must stand up for and represent their entire cultural or ethnic group.

Some women of color rebel against this expectation, while still acknowledging that such an expectation exists and feeling an innate obligation to honor it: if they go to college, they're expected to help and encourage other women in their families and sub-groups to do likewise; if they're successful in business, they're expected to share their wealth and help others to achieve the same level of success that they have. This ensures that women of color do not just experience individual success; instead, mentorship and helping the advancement of others becomes an integral part of their success if they are to be appreciated by the social, ethnic, and cultural group to which they belong.

Hence, while traditional business groups will cater to a monolithic group in which everyone is expected to engage, women's groups will often be segmented not only within a given professional group (i.e., education; IT; finance; business), but also culturally. In 2020, I was invited to speak at a group of female university and college bursars and leaders—so not only were these women in education, but they were a *subset* of women in education.

I live in south Florida, a salad bowl of Caribbean and South and Central American cultures featuring groups not just for black women, but specifically for those of Caribbean (or, even more specifically, Jamaican or Haitian) heritage. All of these groups will hold meetings, conferences, and events geared specifically toward ensuring that women within these cultures are able to be seen, recognized, given advancement opportunities, and pay it forward to members within that cultural group.

This is why we've seen the explosion of hashtags that are not just women-specific, but also smaller-cultural-groups-specific: because this is an inherent part of the BossLadyLeader of color dynamic. Evidently, there are clear cultural lines which have been drawn, despite the typically utopian view being that we are all part of a single group. I was recently watching a mini documentary on Facebook where a group of black Latin women discussed the conundrum they found themselves in: they were both black and Latina, and identified with both groups. Hence, they experienced the discrimination and expectations of both groups. Here, they also discussed their need to have a greater level of visibility so that other black Latinas felt represented within the larger Latina diaspora.

This whole notion of "cultural identity" further confuses the issues for women of color we are going to explore as we move forward; I had huge fights with one of my faculty members when I first discussed my dissertation title, in which I made a very clear distinction between black and African-American women. He dismissed me and told me that this was a single group. Needless to say, he'd just opened the floodgates of my ire, and I (very vociferously!) explained to him that no, they were not; that I was neither African, nor American. The poor man was perplexed, and couldn't understand why I was two-cultured. Just picture me doing a huge eyeroll at this point. I then broke it down to him: I explained that "black" is a race and "African-American" is an ethnicity, and, while I had no issue with being black, my ethnicity was Jamaican, Caribbean, or West Indian. I could pick any of those three.

We continued to argue for a few weeks, but he finally relented when I basically told him that he could not tell me what my ethnicity was.

So, I'm in a position where I do understand why all of these various small groups wish to have a smidgeon of their own identity to cling to—and, because there are very different cultural expectations within these groups, it would suggest that women mentoring women of cultural similarities would experience great success in doing so. I, myself, have mentored two Jamaican women, formally in a professional capacity, later informally; however, now, as a baby entrepreneur, I am seeing a totally different side to this, as many of my mentors are of completely different races and cultures than I am.

My current mentor is within the specified age range to be a successful match—she is 10 years my junior—, but we are from different cultural groups: I'm Jamaican and she's Cuban. Saying this, we do both identify as "island people"; plus, she's the child of immigrants, so we share a similar "immigrant outlook" on the fact that success is something we need to work for. We have a similar worth ethic and parenting styles, and we genuinely like and respect one another. In summary, we have all the criteria required for a successful mentor/mentee relationship, and have even partnered on a business venture, the single goal of which being to create an educational event for women of all cultural backgrounds.

Women of color have an immense burden when it comes to achievement, success, leadership, mentorship, and paying it forward, and within this are the research findings that women (unlike men) will only mentor women who they view as being similar to themselves (and not necessarily just with regard to race). My mentor and I are an example of this: even though I was once her teacher, while I continued on one path, she continued on another—and, while I may be a content expert, I did not have the social media or creative savvy required to implement some of the things I wished to. She, however, had an extensive network she could introduce me to, allowing me to get to the levels of success that I needed to with my fledgling company.

Take my logo, for example: I had my nephew create it, since he's family and has a small company. I wanted to give him some exposure and get him more work in order to grow his company, and, when he was done with it, she saw it and loved the concept, but told me that the font was too masculine. She knew that I wanted a strong, blocky font, and so she simply took the raw files and played around with it until we got to a font that we both liked, only that represented a more feminine aesthetic. She then continued to introduce me to a number of programs and applications I could use to create graphics for my social media.

The role of a mentor is not just to teach you, but also to give you the exposure you need in order to become successful in what you do. I excel at helping women excel within male-dominated cultures because that's what I've done for 20 years, and what *my* mentor excels at is helping individual women understand what they need to do in order to successsssfully promote and grow their own brands.

After we conquered the logo challenge, she introduced me to a network of female entrepreneurs on Facebook—and, within days of joining the group, I was introduced to Notebook Publishing.

That is the epitome of what mentors do: they help to position you for success.

One of the things I've learned in the last 20 years of mentoring and being mentored is that sometimes, we don't realize *when* we are being mentored. Research indicates that many black women in the United States are first led to leadership because of the roles they play at church and within the family—the places where they learn of their own emotional intelligence skills and all the skillsets essential to being a leader. This makes them eminently qualified to then continue to mentor women who are similar to themselves. Indeed, we often do not recognize some of the more informal forms of mentorship that occur in social environments. All of these organizations and clubs that we are involved in were honing leadership skills for years.

When I first became a director at the tender age of 30, two of the other directors (who were at least 10 to 15 years my senior) would often seek me out and have conversations with me. At the time, I didn't really understand the importance of those conversations, but, knowing I was the new kid on the block, they would try to give me the 411 on any given number of things so that I didn't make any of the mistakes they'd made and could be successful in my role. Neither woman, however, came outright and told me, "Hey don't do this, because this will happen"; instead, they engaged in storytelling and recounting events and incidents from previous terms. It was then up to me to interpret the subtext of those stories so as to determine the way in which I would tailor my actions going forward. I knew their goal was to "help me out", but years later, I began to understand how critical their assistance had actually been to my success. Within five years, I would eventually become *their* leader—and I am certain that this would not have come about without the informal mentorship they offered me.

So, we've established how useful and integral storytelling is to women and their mentorship process. The only thing I will say about this tool is that you should be careful to ensure that the storytelling doesn't meander into the area of bragging: it's good to share methods and stories of both success and failure (those are, after all, critical learning experiences), but the storytelling can very quickly adopt the tone of, "This is how I do things", "This is why my way is the best", and "Any other way than mine is stupid." If this becomes the case, we may need to reconsider the whole angle we're approaching our storytelling with.

As a part of mentoring women, I do like to share the times when I, myself, have made bad judgments. One of the stories I tell is that of when I was part of a hiring panel: we were hiring for a leadership position on-campus, and had two candidates: one male, one female. The male candidate rubbed me up the wrong way: he was arrogant and abrasive, and I found him to be offensive. He was hired by the largely male group to work for us and had some success. However, when he was eventually managed by a woman, he was summarily fired due to his inability to work collegially with women. I like to think that I made a good decision about his ability to be successful within the organization.

However, my abysmal failure came with the female: I was utterly and totally bowled over and charmed by her. She looked the part and talked the part, and I immediately felt she was the best thing since sliced bread. Hence, I was certain she'd be invaluable for the role. Fast forward six months, however, and I found that she was sneaky, conniving, a liar, and that she manipulated all situations that came her way to her advantage. Further, during a compliance audit I was running for her location, I found she'd actually had a staff member trail me everywhere I went to attempt to listen in on my phone calls. I was literally in an episode of some crime drama, and I was the perp dodging Five O. At first, I was annoyed—and then that led to borderline hysterical amusement.

Thus, I decided to have some fun with the situation: since we all work for the same organization, there's no need for me to use my cellphone unless the situation is confidential. My email and work line are all accessible, and are all connected once I log into the network—so I waited until my designated spy was in the area and then made a big deal about needing to go outside to make a call. I then darted outside and hid behind a wall, and, when my spy came out of the building and began hunting for me, I magically materialized from behind the wall and slid up to her with my brow quirked, *a la* The Rock, wondering what the heck she was cooking. She had the most comical look on her face when she rounded the corner and found me waiting for her. Once she and I met face-to-face in that moment, she realized the jig was up; then, within earshot, I simply called the President and recounted to her in great detail the cat-and-mouse situation I'd been enduring for the past two days—that is, *after* I was done laughing like a hyena over the whole thing.

The good thing is that this woman eventually resigned from the position: once she realized the entire leadership team in the organization had recognized that she not wasn't competent, but that she also lacked integrity, she decided to exit stage.

Bye, Felicia.

I still consider that to be one of my greatest failures: as a leader and a mentor, I like to consider myself to be a good judge of character, and my inability to see through her fake façade is still one of my greatest failures—I'd honestly thought she'd had all the right ingredients, and that I could mentor her into being successful within our organization.

Because it is essential for potential leaders to understand that you may not always get it right, this is a story I share often. I'm good without about 95% of my hires. I also currently have a great core team who I work with, and I trust them to do their job without being micromanaged. In truth, they boss *me* around quite a bit, telling me what I need to do and when—something that's fine with me! It means I have a team that's a well-oiled machine. However, as individual leaders, we'll make mistakes—and we'll need to own them and then adjust our behaviors accordingly!

One of the things I also learned from one of my team members is that I'm not always the right person to mentor another on the team or an individual. Remember, they boss *me* around. There I was, in my Mentorship Queen bubble, and there she came, raining all over my parade. In my job as Vice President, I'm always available to mentor at many levels of the organization—I should be mentoring anyone who has a regional leadership position—, but there came a time when I found that I was getting more and more frustrated with mentoring a particular individual. I voiced such a frustration to one of my directors, who began to laugh hysterically before calmly telling me that my personality and that of the person in the role would not work together. She also pointed out that my title was also a barrier: he would never challenge me because he viewed me as a superior whose orders he had to follow.

With this in mind, I flipped the script and had her do the mentorship instead. What resulted was the following: she not only was not able to mentor him, but also everyone in that group. This resulted in extraordinary results, including the creation of new, more effective processes and procedures with a superlative work product.

I learned a critical lesson that day: I didn't often see myself in the same way that others did. I saw myself as part of the team, while he saw me as being *above* the team. What that meant was that we were working at cross-purposes and accomplishing little as a result. I was frustrated, and he felt like he was disappointing me. Today, because he sees me in the role he expects, he's able to work much better with me: he sees my director as his mentor and me as the management of the mentor system. Win-win!

I often find myself handing out mentorship advice everywhere I go. I was recently finishing up my lash and eyebrow appointment when I asked my consultant, Shonae, about her apprentice, who I hadn't seen in a while. Her huge sigh and sloping shoulders immediately told me all was not well. Now, my lash consultant and I are both born in September, are Virgos, and are scarily similar: we are both of West Indian heritage (she's half Jamaican and half Barbadian), and have similar outlooks on life, business, parenting, and relationships.

Shonae explained that she wanted to have a conversation with her apprentice because she felt, based on her behavior, that she was not committed to her own personal, professional, or business growth. Shonae was feeling frustrated and let down, and wanted to have a "come to Jesus" conversation with her about her plans. I fully understood her situation: remember, women generally mentor those they see potential in, so seeing your efforts seemingly going to waste is frustrating. Shonae was on the verge of expanding her business, and she needed to determine how much of her time and energy she needed to continue to invest in her apprentice. She was committed, as a woman of color, to helping another woman of color, especially one who was a single parent and wanted to be a beauty entrepreneur.

My advice to Shonae was that she first needed to have the conversation in a neutral place. I explained that having that conversation in her place of business immediately put her in a superior role that would change the tenure of the conversation. I suggested that they meet outside of work at Starbucks or Dunkin Donuts and that this be more of a touch base conversation to see how she was doing, what support she needed, and how she saw herself moving forward in the next few weeks. I explained to Shonae that as a mentor, you need to always approach things from the viewpoint of supporting the mentee. I told her that I understood her frustration and she could share that with me, but not with the mentee. We discussed how she could have this conversation and it not become confrontational.

We did, however, determine that the conversation needed to end with her handing accountability over to her mentee. We discussed that, as a mentor, Shonae would clarify that she'd already fulfilled the time limit criteria they'd established at the start of the mentorship—and that now was the time when she would be expanding her business footprint. As such, she would be taking others under her wing, and so would have less time to spend with her one-on-one. However, she would still attempt to support her as much as she could, even though the initial mentorship period had ended.

Shonae seemed pleased with this avenue of addressing the issue. I explained to her that while mentoring someone is wonderful, her apprentice needed to actually want, appreciate, and participate in the mentorship; that, after all, was the only way that she could or would be successful.

Women of color already have the deck stacked against them in some areas as a result of under-representation and the exclusion we oftentimes face. Add into that the lack of participation in a plan for success, and then you'll find yourself with the recipe for failure. Hence, it is absolutely critical that if you're going to mentor someone, that your mentee is worthy of the time you're going to be investing into them—and also that they *want* to be successful and are willing to put in the work and sacrifice necessary to achieve such success. My mother always told me to not want anything for anyone that they did not want for themselves: that only leads to your own heartbreak and disappointment.

Now, here's the other big issue mentors often face when working with women of color: the many naysayers and haters who out there waiting to tell you that you cannot succeed and need to stay in your lane; that you should stop "trying to be white and better than everybody else", and just accept the status quo. This is because society is inherently structured to *not* help us be successful. This is, of course, a very strong message, and is essentially echoed at you over and over again.

It's so loud that it can sometimes drown out that small voice inside you that reminds you that this is your dream; that this is what God means and needs for you to do; that this is the path you need to be on. This is the Demon of Self-Doubt, accompanied by the Hell Hounds of Haterators.

Self-doubt is the first cousin of imposter syndrome: they exist side-by-side and provide one another with their much-needed oxygen. I'm not sure which comes first, but they both sit there egging each other on, and are each a thorn in the side of those of us who just want to mentor women to success in peace. In the case of my consultant's apprentice, I don't believe the issue was imposter syndrome: the beauty industry is extremely easy for women of color to enter and excel in, since they spend much more money and time on beauty than other demographics. Hence, it's a sure way for a female entrepreneur to be successful.

If, however, there's a woman of color from an environment where she's never seen a woman excel in a job (even if it's her own business), then this doesn't seem like something she can achieve—and even when she's being mentored by another woman of color, she still sees this as something that may not be achievable: all she sees is the woman standing in her own salon. She doesn't see the years of struggle and sacrifice that allows the successful woman to have her name on a door—and, *because* she's not seeing the step-by-step struggle and where that struggle can lead, she'll find every possible reason to justify her lack of success or unwillingness to put forth any sacrifices herself. She can't do it because of her kids; she can't do it because of her life partner; she can't do it because of her parents; she can't do it because the sun may rise tomorrow. No matter what, there'll always be a myriad of excuses as to why success is not possible.

This self-doubt will take root, and then those haterators around her will hone in on this self-doubt like a heat-seeking missile and confirm all the reasons why success is not possible for her. Misery loves company, and they do not want to see her successful: her success would put their own lack of success into sharp focus, and introspection into their situation is really not on the menu. What *is* on the menu is ensuring that she has so much self-doubt and lack of faith in herself that she will abandon the project of her awareness and personal and professional growth altogether.

We discussed imposter syndrome previously, as well as the system I have in place in order to manage this in a more corporate setting. When I'm working with a woman in a corporate environment, this is easy to do: I can work with her each day and be the voice drowning out the naysayers and haterators. However, in the case of my consultant, she didn't know what her apprentice went home to each evening, and relied on calls to ensure that she kept in touch.

One of the things women of color need within the mentoring process is a consistent and ongoing presence, and this is even *more* important for those who are starting or trying to grow a business and be an entrepreneur. Women of color often have less access to lines of credit than other women, meaning they are often unable to hire help or have money to do some of the things necessary for a successful business. As such, they face higher stress levels as a result of having to juggle a full-time job and a side-hustle, all while often being parents, significant others, and caretakers of parents.

I really did not understand the stress of making the plunge of leaving your safe and secure job to start your own business, and, being honest, I *still* don't—and that's because I've not yet taken that plunge. When I'm asked why I haven't quit my job to dedicate all my time to my business, I smile: I love my job and what I do, and the only way to do it is within the confines of a college or university. The parts of myself that I don't get to fulfill in my 9 to 5 are the parts that are my business—so my 9 to 5 and side-hustle together leave me a happy, fulfilled person. Giving up one would leave me feeling lost, especially when there's still so much within that field I'd like to do.

With that in mind, I tip my hat to all the women who've taken that great leap and had to make it work because they had no choice but to be exceptional BossLadyleaders.

In 2018, I went to the Essence Festival in New Orleans and had the opportunity to watch a *She Did That* documentary about black female entrepreneurs. This was an eye-opener for me in terms of the struggles women of color face when starting a business: many have solid plans and a small amount of cash that can quickly be depleted if they're not immediately successful. Plus, it's no secret that people of color don't have pockets as deep as others—and many women of color also don't have family who can extend them loans or credit to get the necessary cash to open and keep a business afloat *without* requiring a regular job. Indeed, many women of color run their businesses from their home for many years before they have enough cashflow to afford storefronts, factory space, and all the other things some people take for granted when starting a business.

The documentary showcased a now-highly successful business owner who was laughed off *Shark Tank* with the lipstick line she wanted to carry. Very often, women of color are seeking to start a business that is personal to their own experience and caters to a demographic they know well—and if that's not a demographic that is seen as valuable to the majority (or, rather, those who hold the purse strings), then women of color have no avenue to take but to wait and take it slow. Carol's Daughter was run out of Lisa Davis's home for the first five years of the business.

I'm still in the infancy of my own journey, and I'm looking forward to seeing where this goes. I launched Dr. Sue Speaks in August of 2019, and now, at 9:51pm on December 26th, 2019, I've been able to get one good paying client (the check is literally in the mail), and I'm working on this book, with a second one planned. I also have a #BossLady conference I'm working on, too, which we host in September 2020. I'm not as focused on profit as I possibly could be—I'm focused on brand-building—, but I'm fully cognizant of the fact that I will need to "hit or get off the pot" at some point and make this a profitable venture.

Group Mentorship and Squad Creation

Sometimes, mentorship can be difficult in a one-on-one environment—and, in such situations, it may be that better results would be reached if such a mentorship were to occur within a group setting. There's something powerful about a group of women and what they can achieve: if men were running PTAs and fundraisers, schools would never raise a dime, but get a group of women together and they can raise oodles of money and get almost anything accomplished. Women can accomplish this same thing if mentorship is done at a group level.

My son is a wrestler, and I would soon realize that all the sports gear available is made for men. Each year, his school has a huge fundraising wrestling tournament, and this year, I worked at the door of the tournament, collecting entry fees. I noticed that one of the mothers of a rival wrestling team had bedazzled t-shirts emblazoned with their son's team name, and I was instantly jealous, wondering if we, too, should have similar shirts. So, a group of us mothers got together and went to talk with the coach. He gave us the runaround, and so I opted to simply circumvent him and get to the end goal: vneck women's shirts clearly stating that we were wrestling moms.

Two of us began getting quotes. I immediately contacted Lulu (my mentor of color) and asked her for her connections—and, within two days, I had two designs and pricing. I then sent a note out to all the parents, and 48 hours later, had an order of 22 shirts. The other mom, who was also working on a quote, was actively seeking similar shirts, but this time with crystals. The moral of this story: once women decide on a goal and collaborate, they ultimately achieve the goals they create—even if it's creating t-shirts to support our wrestlers at tournaments!

Women are, by nature, social creatures, and we have been socialized to communicate and collaborate constantly. These traits provide fertile ground for group mentorship. There are a number of meet-up groups, and all it takes is simply downloading a meet-up app, finding out your preferences, waiting for the notifications to hit your email, and then simply going to a meeting. If, however, you're the type to organize, then creating your own group is something that could and would be beneficial to women—especially fellow women of color who are all experiencing the same trials and tribulations in their leadership or entrepreneurship journeys.

There are a number of online groups I've found to be invaluable in helping me, but the greatest help has come about on the occasions when someone is speaking to me one-on-one and addressing my specific situation, providing answers to the problems that I'm experiencing right then and there. Because of this, I can only imagine that other women would want exactly the same thing that I find to be most useful and helpful!

Years ago, I was part of a group of Island Women of Color (black, mixed, Chinese, and Indian) who got together every two or three months for a wine and cheese soiree. It started with just four of us, each of which bringing a bottle of wine and some snacks before sitting down and chatting. It was great. We left spouses, jobs, and children behind to just have one afternoon of fun with other women. Over the next few meetings, which we now alternated between two homes, we expanded that to involve more and more women—which of course meant more and more food and more and more wine. No judging!

Then, one of the ladies in the group suggested we focus the meeting around helping each of us connect with some of the inherent issues with being women—so we were doing wine and cheese with a purpose! We'd found that just the four of us talking about the issues we were having and getting some feedback had been immensely helpful, so we wanted to do this on a larger scale. The planner in our group went online and found questions, wrote them on pieces of paper, and dumped them all into a bowl, and at the next soiree, we each took turns taking a question from the bowl and answering it, before the rest of the women would offer their own thoughts. The format proved to be quite cathartic and eye-opening, and the women quickly became very honest and open about their feelings and issues. We tackled things like accepting compliments and praise, supporting other women who were struggling with issues, being more spiritual and embracing faith in our lives, and asking for help when needed.

We would eventually disband after about 18 months as a result of everyone getting busy, but we helped one of the members through cancer treatments and her eventual marriage to her long-term partner, as well as another through infidelity, parent-child issues, a relationship breakup, and subsequent reunion. While any one of us could help one another through their difficulties, the group dynamic, with multiple people contributing in an environment of confidence, helped some of the women explore topics they never had before, in turn getting them to a better place of understanding and healing. The good food and copious amounts of wine we consumed might have also had a hand in the sharing, but regardless, it was a cathartic and invigorating experience. I miss that group, and one of my goals for 2020 is to go back to more of those social meetups with women.

So, what does this look like as a mentor who's wishing to group mentor a group of women of color?

- **Create a meeting place that is consistent.** It can be someone's home, or a public space, like a library that allows you to bring snacks.
- **Nibbles are always a good idea.** There's a certain camaraderie that happens when people eat together!
- **Schedule monthly meetings.** Not every meeting, however, should be an accountability meeting; there

should be fun meetups (e.g., guest presenters; brunch; painting parties; tours; etc.).

- **Set up a group thread so that members can communicate with one another.** Private groups can be created on Facebook, or use Whatsapp/text threads.
- **Initial meetings should focus on each member's goals for being in the group.**
- **As the mentor, you'll be touching base with each of the members weekly.**
- **A Google document can be created to help keep members accountable to the goals they have set out for themselves.**

The goal of the group is to have a supportive, safe place for each of the mentees; a place where they can share the successes and failures they're currently having. This is also a space where each woman can be with other women experiencing similar challenges with them and discuss how they are managing the fiscal, emotional, and psychological stress of attempting to enter the land of BossLadyhood. In addition to the social aspects of the group, the group can choose to attend conferences and meetings for the sole purpose of enhancing their goals and businesses, allowing for a sense of camaraderie where they don't feel so alone when going to a meeting.

Another thing that will be immeasurably helpful and useful to the mentorship group is inviting successful women in your sphere to come and talk with these women about topics that are of interest to them. Do you have friends in marketing, social media, accounting, goal-setting, HR, or even insurance? All these are areas that budding leaders and entrepreneurs need to understand if they're to be successful in their own endeavors. The week before you're due to have one of your colleagues address your group, ask the members to gather their questions to give to the guest speaker ahead of time. The guest speaker will now have a good idea of the group and what their needs are, which will make her even *more* useful to the group: she can now give targeted answers, and everyone's needs can be met. This is also a mini networking event, since now, the mentees have yet another #BossLady they've met.

Creating and Maintaining Accountability in Mentoring

Earlier, I discussed how I'd been ABD (All But Dissertation) with my doctorate: I essentially dropped out of school for two years, and I'll be honest, I didn't really have much remorse about it. My rationalization at the time was that I was already a Vice President, so how was a mere doctorate going to help me? I was already at the highest point that I wanted to get to in the education industry! Back in 2011, the thought of opening a business was nowhere on my radar. Thought Leadership? What's *that*? And why on earth would I want to do it? You mean create a business that requires I work nine to 10 hours each day, only to come home and do *more*? Are you nuts? Well, apparently, I am, because here I am nine years later being all Thought Leader with my own company.

But the reason I had the *option* to be ABD was because I had no accountability. Now, don't get me wrong, Argosy University and their Student Counseling Department were certainly *trying* to keep me accountable: that poor man (God bless his heart) would call me at least once a week and send me emails, and I would consistently send him to voicemail and ignore his pleas. So, even as a leader, I fully understand the mentality that goes into choosing not to finish a project, or choosing to fail at something because actually doing the work didn't fit your current narrative. My own excuses went like this:

- I already have a leadership job.
- The degree isn't going to make me any more money.
- I'm too busy.
- I don't feel like writing a book.
- I hate statistics.

So, now, whenever I'm working with a woman and I hear these excuses, I smile: been there, done that, have the t-shirt!

What spurred me on to actually complete my degree was believing that I was somehow going to be a disappointment to my son for being a "quitter", as his dad ever-so-eloquently said, or that my family would be disappointed in me for not being all I could be. How could I be fighting for women's benefits while my job was here, paying for my degree, and I was still squandering the opportunity? Remember, as a woman of color, I carry the honor of my family and all black and Jamaican women in my DNA—so back to school I went to complete what I'd started!

I'd initially joined a doctoral accountability group on Facebook, but I was not really into Facebook groups back then and so found such a method didn't work for me. It's really important for each mentor and mentee to find what the best accountability tool for them iss. Group accountability is not a good option for me personally, but I've worked with lots of women—especially those who are naturally competitive— who find group accountability to be great. I've found that women who work in any sales-related activity tend to enjoy group accountability, especially if linked to kudos and recognition of accomplishment.

On the other hand, you have people like me: those who are fairly good at holding themselves accountable, but do well with one person reminding them of their ultimate goal, providing gentle nudges in the direction they need to go in. Enter Lulu: she has been urging me to go to meetings and network more—something that's in my planner to sort out. 2019 was the first time in years that I'd kept a planner: I got one in my Singles Swag Box (yes, I was married, but I love that monthly box; no judging!) in 2018, and it was a lifesaver in 2019.

My initial plan was to be all plannerific and do stickers and have one of those beautiful pictorial planners—but that didn't happen! You've seen those elaborate planner pages on Instagram. They're beautiful: a mix of graphic design and scrapbooking. Maybe one day I'll get there, but that day is *not*

today (and wasn't any day in 2019, for that matter!). We can keep hope alive for 2020, though. So, instead of plannerificness, I kept a basic planner with a few stickers that had all the pertinent dates

recorded. I quickly realized that even though I'd quickly be kicked out of any planner group for my lack of creativity or attempts to be plannerific, I was so much more organized with everything in my planner (i.e., my personal schedule and appointments; holidays; business meetings; events; my son and his dad's schedules; social events).

It was then that Lulu stepped it up and said that I needed to get a *wall* planner, so that I could see my entire month at a time and where I had gaps and opportunities to book other things in. By this time, she and I had both acknowledged that I'd be writing this book, so I needed to plan my writing time around the meetups, as well as my regular life. Hence, one night, as I was thinking about what I needed to do, I jumped onto Amazon and found a design I liked and ordered it. Two days later, it came, and by December 23rd, 2019, I already had all my appointments and meet-ups for January and February in both my planners. I still have my Singles Swag planner (yup, I got my 2020 one in my December box, and I love it), and that one is kept in my purse with a duplicate on my wall. The good thing is that because I'm planning to be more active with my business in 2020, this also allows my family to know what I'm doing—so, if it's 7pm and they don't see me at home, they can easily see if I've snuck off to a local meet-up, network meeting, or business mixer.

Accountability is a critical part of mentorship, and is as individual as the women of color you are mentoring. If you're reading this book because you're a BossLady wanting to create other BossLadies, then just remember that you'll need to tailor your mentorship to each of the ladies you mentor; and, if you're a BossLady seeking to move *yourself* to leadership, then you need to figure out what the best way for your mentor and you to keep yourself accountable is.

Mentoring is a personal exercise, and is not a one-size-fits-all endeavor: in fact, the older I get, the more I realize that *nothing* is one-size-fits-all; that, at least, is a tool we've finally realized doesn't work!

One day, I was listening to the radio and heard Kane 11 advertising men's socks that came in sizes 6 to 12 for women and 7 to 17 for men, and I realized that the world was coming to the same realization. But isn't that logical? We buy shoes in sizes, so why not socks? Then when the Third Love bramakers created half sizes of bras, I realized that the world was finally getting it right: if we could make socks in individual sizes, then we could certainly create a garment where our breasts were properly accommodated! It's all about the uniqueness of the fit.

As we can see from the above, we need to cater to all people's nuances and not try to shove everyone into neatly labeled boxes that ultimately *don't* cater to individual needs. We're all different and need different things to be motivated and succeed, after all—and the key is finding what that thing is, and then just keep doing what you need to do until you get to the point that you want to get to. And trust me, I know that this is easier said than done: the will is often not as strong as we need it to be. We often feel disheartened, depressed, and downtrodden when things aren't always going our way and we meet roadblock after roadblock. However, the goal is to always be moving forward, because staying still is really never an option! This is why a mentorship and accountability plan for women of color will need to accommodate and account for the unique challenges that women of color specifically face.

SELF-REVIEW TIME

Things I learned in this chapter...

_____

_____

_____

What I may do differently now that I understand more about mentorship...

_____

_____

_____

Do I need a mentor?

_____

_____

What would I need from a mentor?

_____

_____

_____

Do I think I can mentor another woman?

_____

_____

_____

What can I offer a mentee?

_____

_____

_____

Notes

_____

_____

_____

_____

_____

_____

_____

_____

_____

CHAPTER 6:
LEVEL UP YOUR GAME -
ACHIEVING BOSSLADYSHIP

S O, NOW WE GET to the most important part of this book. For the last four chapters, we've taken you on a journey of self-realization and actualization by taking a look at yourself and ensuring that you're ready for the challenges of being a leader, as well as for overcoming the negative internal and external voices around you so you're in a position to achieve the goals you've established for yourself. Once you're at this point, you're officially able to take on whatever challenges you encounter. You now have the tools and information you need in order to aim for that promotion, or to resign from your job because you plan to become a BossLady CEO.

What Is BossLadyShip?

We've talked for four chapters about BossLadyShip, but what is it exactly? BossLadyShip is the ability and skill to take on a leadership role in any scenario that you so happen to find yourself in; it allows you to take on leadership roles in your corporate environment, to lead your non-profit to meeting its goals, to start and/or grow your business, and to take on the helm of being the CEO of your home, if your chosen vocation is that of a homemaker. The same skills apply in any of these scenarios: BossLadyShip and leadership are mirror twins of one another, the single difference being that BossLadyShip centres on understanding the inherent challenges women experience when embarking upon leadership. This is then further compounded by the further challenges faced by women of color specifically.

Followers Make Leaders

My doctorate is in Organizational Leadership, and people mistakenly believe that because I have such an education, this automatically makes me a leader—but it does not! Leadership is defined by a single fact: you can only lead when people choose to follow you. People often mistake management for leadership: with management, you can tell people what to do, and they follow your directives—but it's not leadership. So, ladies of color, know that you achieve BossLadyShip when people believe in what you're saying, doing, and selling, and *then* choose to engage with you.

So, have a clear platform and set of ideals that guide your actions, thoughts, and business goals, because once you do that, everybody is very clear about your standards. It is, however, incumbent upon you to make sure that you understand those you are seeking to engage with.

I was working with a retail client who only carried clothes made by women here in the United States with good-quality fabric. These are all exemplary standards. However, there is a price point associated with such a high-quality product, and this was not a price point her clients were willing to pay. Hence, in order to move her product, she always ended up having to put the items on sale, thereby cutting into her profit margin. In my consultation with her, I showed her how several other boutiques were selling similar products—albeit not the same quality—, but were undercutting her prices by sometimes 40%-60%. She was not achieving BossLadyShip because she was making a cardinal mistake: failing to understand her followers and demographic.

In order to lead, you must first know how to follow. When you understand the feelings and motivations of those whom you want to impact, then it's that much easier for you to create solutions, plans, programs, products, and messages that appeal to your demographic. This is why being a BossLady gives you an immediate advantage when working with other women: you understand those women, their motivations, and what they're most likely to do, because you, too, are a woman. This is even more poignant when you're a woman of color, especially if you're part of a subculture (e.g., Caribbean; West Indian; black Hispanic/Latina; black Jewish; mutli-ethnic; muti-racial; transgender; Muslim; etc.); here, You have an even keener understanding of what it means to exist within this sub-group and the special marketing, words, phrases, and strategies that will allow you to be successful within your demographic.

The Likeability Factor

Here's the bottom line: people only follow people they like and respect. It's really that simple. Hence, your goal in BossLadyShip is to ensure that you're likeable and that you do nothing to erode that likeability/respect people have in your skill, ability, integrity, or ethics. Now, for women, this is a double-edged sword: there are societal constraints on how women should behave in order to be successful, and yet there is a level of arrogance and aggressiveness that is needed in business—something that is frowned upon for women in society.

Because the majority culture doesn't appreciate when women take on roles traditionally held by men, black women often face the moniker of being loud, ghetto, overly aggressive, or bossy when taking on BossLadyShip—and, because of this, many black women have had to learn how to temper their natural BossLady behaviors in order to maintain the likeability factor so as to accomplish their goals. Our Latina sisters face similar trials: they're seen as hot-headed and overly emotional when they feel passionately about an issue and address it; and our Asian sisters face a similar story in which they are often fetishized as timid, docile, and thus unable to lead.

Hence, in order for women to take on a bigger, more influential role in the shaping of business and the direction of this nation, all women (and all women of color) must stand together in support of one another. Indeed, there continue to be divisions between women, and even between women of color. On this note, one of the respondents who considered herself to be mixed said the following during the interview process:

The hardest challenge was not taking the various types of prejudices from other women of color personally. Most of the prejudices occurred during my early professional life, and it was from one ethnic group: African-American. Once I understood the sub-culture and/or the personality type, it was easy not to take the prejudices personally. Another contributing factor was I was determined to succeed, so I just remained focused. My determination to succeed exposed me to multiple mentors throughout my professional career. Funnily, none of my mentors were people of color.

—Sherrie, Plantation, FL

This is just one glaring example of how women of color need to get together and have conversations about how to compromise on any number of issues; this is all in pursuit of ensuring that everyone has a clear understanding of how to move forward harmoniously.

As a young professional, one of the things I noticed was that there was never a plan to mitigate personality differences with men in the organization; instead, it was a given that men were level-headed and knew how to work through personality conflicts. However, there *were* very specific plans on how to address personality conflicts and differences between women, which, to me, did not aid in women in growing into BossLeaders within the organization. Now, if I'm honest, I bought into this stereotype until I did a self-audit and realized that this belief system was really not conducive to me being an effective leader: here, I realized that in doing so, I was essentially buying into the belief that women are unable to self-regulate and thus have no self-control/autonomy, and need to be controlled like children.

I had to realize and acknowledge that *I* was part of the issue. Each person (and thus, each woman) needed to be assessed on their own merit. What made me a BossLeader was my ability to recognize the talents and skills each person brought to the table—and then ensuring that those talents and skills were aligned with the desired organizational outcomes/personal goals. As a BossLeader, I do believe that it's criticial that I especially seek out those who are like me— that, is, who may be overlooked within an organization—, and ensure that they *do* have the ability to shine.

Now, one of the things that came out of my doctoral research was that women are very stingy about who and how they mentor: women are willing to mentor, but they only choose to mentor those they already see as having the possibility of success. This is also prevalent with BossLeaders who are black: black women are unwilling to mentor those who they don't see as having the potential to be successful, seeing anything to be a waste of their time other than mentoring those they can see have the ability to be successful, and/or those who it would be directly advantageous to the organization.

I previously discussed the conversation I had with my lash consultant, Shonae, who was working with her mentee—and, when I followed up with her three weeks later to determine how the meeting had gone, she immediately said she'd severed the relationship: the mentee didn't have the right attitude to become a BossLady, and was indulging in poor planning and lack of vision.

If you're a BabyBossLady or a BossLady in training looking for a mentor, it's really important that you exhibit all the right traits to be seen as a good option to be taken on for mentorship:

1. Professionalism.
2. Curiosity.
3. Natural talent and skill.
4. Understanding in the fact that everything is a process, and a willingness to respect the process.
5. Respect for your mentor's time and ability.

Empathy and Understanding

We've discussed empathy before in the context of it being a part of emotional intelligence, and I'll mention it again here as a critical element of BossLadyShip. You must always understand the demographic you're marketing to, as well as those you're managing and leading. For many years, I went to a female gynecologist for one reason: I figured if I was going to go to a doctor about my lady parts, then I should go to someone who actually *had* lady parts. I also read that women who had female doctors got better care. I've had a male doctor for the last few years and it's worked out well, but my conversations with him are vastly different from the ones with my female physician, simply because we're two women versus my talking to my male caregiver. It's different. Not bad; just different.

It's critical that, as a BossLady of color, you have some empathy for those who are similar to you. I've already discussed our prejudice with mentorship and others who are similar, but if you're just aware of the choices you can make and not allow prejudices or preconceived notions to make your decisions, that will be a plus in the column of your achievement of BossLadyShip.

Trust, Integrity, and Accountability

Now, I know it sounds like BossLadies are running for politics because of all the traits they need to have and exhibit, but these three are the trifecta of necessity; without them, you can never, *ever* be a BossLady or BossLeader. These three elements are critical to the success of any person individually, to the growth of an organization, and/or for the establishment of your business and the building of your brand. It just takes one small issue for a brand to be tarnished, and so it's important that BossLadies do not do anything to tarnish their image.

a. **Within an Organization**

When you want to increase your sphere of influence within your organization, you need to ensure that those you lead and manage, as well as those who lead and manage you, need to i) trust your choices and actions, ii) know that you operate at the highest level of integrity (because managers do things right while leaders do the right thing), and iii) know that as a BossLady, you have a high level of accountability—not only for yourself, but also for those you manage and lead.

b. **Within your Business**

When you're seeking to start your business or grow your business, your clients need to trust the products and the services you offer—meaning that you maintain the quality of the product, are honest and truthful about the services you offer, and then deliver whatever it is that you state that you plan to deliver. In today's world of Google, Amazon, and Yelp reviews, it's never a good idea to do anything that allows people to question/tarnish your name due to the integrity/quality of your product and/or service being called into question.

c. **Building your Brand**
   This simply builds on the aforementioned points, but I choose to discuss this separately because, in today's Facebook and Instagram world, branding has become paramount. Everybody is able to make money based on the believability, integrity, and trust that is placed in a given brand—and if as an individual or someone within your sphere of influence calls any of that into question, that immediately tarnishes your brand—which, in turn, has a negative impact on your ability to secure resources and increase your bottom line.

Stepping Out in Faith

Even those who are non-religious use this saying, because sometimes, that is exactly what you're doing. Anyone who owns a business knows that starting a business is a huge gamble and risk. Remember what I was told when I created my LLC? The government gives you five years to have a hobby—so even the government is aware that it takes time, energy, and resources to make any business successful (and gives you five years to do that). According to the Small Business Association, 30% of new businesses will fail within the first two years of opening, 50% in the first five years, and 66% in the first 10 years.

This is already a daunting number, but BossLadies need to know the things they can do in order to prevent this and have a greater level of success:

- **Have strong management and leadership skills**. This book has already told you all the things you need to do here—so just do them.

- **Find your niche.** There's no sense in going out there and opening up the fortieth nail salon in a town of 500 people—and if you do, what sets your salon apart from the others?

- **Understand your peeps.** You must cater to your demographic. BossLadyShip—especially BossLadyShip of color—means you've done copious amounts of research on your target audience and know everything about them so that you understand their wants and needs and can tailor your product or service to them. That's the advantage ladies of color have over other groups: a greater understanding of the demographic.

- **Get a good accountant and financial manager.** If money management isn't your thing, then get help. There's no shame when it comes to becoming and staying successful! Get whatever help you need in order to be (and stay) successful. Many BossLadies of color understand that they're setting the blueprint for those to come, so set a good blueprint! If you squander your resources and the business closes, then others looking on will feel it's not possible for them, either.

- **Slow your roll!** Growing up in Jamaica, we have an extremely large Chinese population: the Chinese came to Jamaica in the 19th century and established themselves as part of the merchant class. Almost all supermarkets are owned by Chinese families, and they have, over time, moved from simple corner shops into not just large supermarkets, some individuals owning multiple stores and chains. The saying that Jamaicans have about Chinese families is that they start their stores by all living above the shop, and that when you see them either expand the store or buy a house, they can buy and build not just one, but 10. The lesson in that is that they learned to not grow too quickly: instead, they would pace themselves, and when they *did* choose to expand, they had the capital and human resources necessary in order to be able to grow and expand efficiently and effectively.

But you have been reading this book and doing all the work you need already, so you've got this! Now, all you need to do is level up your game of BossLadyShip: trust that you have the knowledge and skill to do this thing, and then just go do the thing!

Be Courageous

Courage and fearlessness are not things we've discussed before, but fearlessness is a hallmark of leadership—and, thus, BossLadyShip. For my entrepreneur BossLadies, you have to be willing to take some risks. Now, no one is saying to bungee jump without checking the rope; instead, you need to take calculated risks: look at the pros and cons, talk with your financial planner, review your resources, and see if there are scenarios out there for you to take advantage of. Being a first adopter of anything is scary, but there are always greater rewards for those who get on the bandwagon first than those who get on tenth.

Saying this, remember all the work you've done thus far. Go back and re-read the self-audit chapters and know that you're ready and prepared to take this leap of faith to accomplish the goals you've laid out for yourself. I love those memes out there about our comfort zones; they're all so accurate! The one that I love the most is, "Innovation happens outside of your comfort zone." Nothing worth accomplishing is ever going to be easy; rather, it's going to require some level of discomfort and stretching your norms until the stretch becomes your new normal—and that's okay! It's all part of the growth process.

What I've found, being a woman of color, is that I have a level of flexibility with doing things that other women don't have: there are less expectations of me that I need to adhere to, which has allowed me to break some rules and create a space for myself where no one holds any expectations. As a matter of fact, by the time they've realized I'd carved out a niche for myself, I'm already comfortably residing there and have created a new normal for everyone! Hence, being a woman of color allowed me to color (pun intended!) outside the lines and have the courage to try something new—mostly because the majority groups had no expectations of me, but my friends and family did. They expected me to find a way to make it happen, so I did!

Continuous Learning

In the self-audit, we discussed education at length in order to fill any gaps in your BossLadyShip knowledge base—but this is not a one and done. I'm a strong advocate of being a continuous learner: I'm all about always reading, watching documentaries, going to seminars, and increasing your knowledge base. I've found that the best way for me to increase my knowledge is to simply talk to people: if I go to a conference, I talk to people and always end up learning something new. I read a lot for work between policy, emails, and articles, so I'm always learning that way, too. I've found LinkedIn to be a great way to keep abreast of a number of different industries and topics, as well as to meet new people and professionals.

I've not embarked upon taking a formal educational course in about two or three years, so I'm due for one soon;

however, launching my business has meant that I've spent a lot of time talking with other entrepreneurs and marketing specialists in order for me to move my business forward. I'm writing this book a mere six months into launching my business, so I'm a neophyte business owner, and have a lot to learn myself about entrepreneurship—but even still, I've met and worked with many successful business owners, and one of the things I know is that they, too, are always learning.

One of the friends that I've known forever is a self-employed aesthetician, and I've always been impressed by how much time she spends on the continual education of herself. She's been an aesthetician for over 30 years now, so the question many would ask her would be whether there even is anything else to know. She still lives in Jamaica and travels to the US at least once a year—sometimes twice to attend conferences. At first, I thought it was really about the products, but she gets the program months in advance so that she can review all the classes available. This is with the aim of determining how she can get her learning on way in advance. So, even with as many years in the business as she has, she's always willing to find something new to learn that can help her in her business.

She's the model for all successful BossLady entrepreneurs: not only do they need to learn about their core product, but about the industry standards and norms that could impact the business, or changing of the economic landscape and tax structures. All of these things can either negatively or positively impact a business, and are thus critical elements of education that a BossLady needs to maintain. A BossLady must also be a student of human nature: we've already discussed emotional intelligence, as well as empathy. The ability to successfully employ and deploy these two skillsets are the pieces of human nature that are the cornerstones of BossLadyShip success.

Functional and Structural BossLadyShip

For any BossLady to be successful, she must be both people- and process-oriented. We just discussed being a student of human nature, and this goes a long way in being successful when it comes to being people-oriented, as this means understanding how people think, act, and react so you are able to manage and lead them effectively (or provide them with desired products and services).

I hope you're now seeing how all the things we've been discussing are all part of your BossLadyShip bag of tricks!

Being process-oriented, on the other hand, means having efficient and effective methods for doing things that get you to your end game and will yield success. Many women of color are parts of microcultures, and many microcultures will have unique ways of doing things; however, it's important that you understand what parts of your culture you need to fold in, and which you don't. The Caribbean culture, for example, is one that believes that if you have a business, then a family member or friend should somehow receive it for free or at a discounted rate if they want to partake in your product or service. Many Caribbean women of color have found this cultural phenomenon to be something that is counterproductive to the success of their business; in fact, many women see this as a method to devalue them and their business, and deeply resent when they are asked to devalue themselves and their product. In fact, some women of color will refuse to work with some demographics because of the prevalence of always wanting a discount or a free service. On a personal note, I've often been asked if I have the "hookup" when discussing with others my side-hustle before I was officially a business.

Two things occur when this happens: the first is a deep feeling of sadness, because you know they'd never ask a man (or someone not of their own race or culture) this question. You realize that this is a blatant way of saying that the only way I'm going to support you is if you make it worth my while. The second is a sense of betrayal: you expect those you're similar to to be more supportive of you and your business. This, however, is where you'll need to put on your big girl panties and address the issue head-on. There are a myriad of ways to do this, but all involve standing up for yourself and ensuring that the party understands that you value yourself, your business, and your product and service. This is also a teachable moment to the party to help to educate them about why their behavior is not helpful and/or respectful.

I've had to deal with people in my race and culture devaluing my products and services by often expecting a"'discount".

—Evon, Lauderhill, FL

There is also a lack of respect for some professions (e.g., those in personal services, like hair and nails). I rarely see this in white salons—and even less in Latina and Hispanic salons—, but this is quite prevalent in black salons. These women are forced to suffer broken appointments or not being paid the full fee for their services. This lack of respect is something that many women of color I know struggle with within their businesses. One such provider, however, uses the style seat app, which requires that all appointments be made online (thereby freeing up the consultant's personal time), the appointment only being made when secured by a credit card. The app sends out reminders about appointments via text at least 24 hours in advance, so there's no excuse about forgetting. It also gives the consultant redress if an appointment is not cancelled and missed because they can still get payment for the time slot which now represents zero revenue for them.

Another one of my retail clients (her customers are largely Hispanic and Brazilian) recently told me about the Sezzle app, which allows people to buy over time. Say you have a product you're selling but your customer doesn't have all the money now: they can pay interest-free over six weeks. It's essentially an installment payment plan app. What this has circumvented for her is people saying they don't have the money, and can they get a discount; now, she can get the full revenue, even though it's over a long period of time.

Both these BossLadies have found processes that are allowing them to sidestep some of the cultural issues that could plague some other business owners, and allows them to keep their clients accountable and realize their full profitability. They don't have to devalue their business or products to make customers happy. Hence, depending on the business you're in, you need processes that allow you to be able to function at full tilt while also understanding your demographic and making some allowances for them.

Communication

Now, along with being people- and process-oriented, we're going back to discussing communication. I cannot stress how important communication is to BossLadyShip; after all, we've discussed it in almost every chapter! Thus, without further ado, here are the communication rules for BossLadyShip:

- Say what you mean and mean what you say.
- Underpromise and overdeliver.
- Do not use false or deceptive language.
- Use positive language in written communication when working with anyone and when interacting with clients and customers.
- Never ever say bad things about competitors.

- Keep your cool when potential customers and/or clients are negative or nasty.
- Have your policies in writing so they are clear. I'm a fan of retailers putting their policies on the receipt; so I know my rights and your rules.

The Rule of the Peter Principle

Lawrence J. Peter wrote a book all the way back in 1969 that discussed people and their rise to the level of their incompetence. Simply put, we cannot be good at everything, and BossLadyLeaders need to know where their weaknesses lie and find a way to fill those areas. Eventually, you'll take on more and more, and some of the things will not be in areas of your expertise—and you'll eventually fail, as you lack competence in that area.

In the field of education, we're constantly looking at data to determine what works, what doesn't, and what the steps we need to make to fix what's wrong are. I love data; I hate *gathering* data! So, years ago, I hired my weakness: a librarian who would eventually become a mini me. Over the last eight years, she has systematically taken over several tasks which I a) don't like, b) require a lot of research to maintain, and c) require ongoing maintenance. Yay, Heather!

As a leader and mentor, one of the things I talk about constantly when working with other mangers and leaders is hiring to plug your weakness. In the corporate world, you hire to backfill areas within an organization; either that, or you do lateral transfers and find people in the organization who can perform the needed tasks. In the entrepreneurial world, however, you have to figure out what isn't working for you, and then see how you can solve the issue. The fabulous thing about it being 2020 is that there is an app or software for everything: there are software programs that help manage the financial side of the business, the human resources side of the business, and even the social media and training side of the business. No longer does a BossLady need to know everything about everything; instead, she needs to know how to access information that allows her to employ the best tools and resources for her business!

Architect of Your Own Success

At the end of the day, you'll need to be the architect of your own success. You're the only one who can take action on the items written on these pages and make them a reality, so you're going to have to take responsibility for both the things that you do and the things that you don't do. Being a woman of color is simply a fact: it's just one of the things that you are. You're more than just a checked box; you're a fully developed person, with talents and skills which you can employ for the advancement of your business or your organization. So you need to fully embrace this notion!

I find I've had less challenges, simply because I didn't expect any. When fellow women in the same profession as I was complained of bias, I had to defer, since I never experienced it from the same people they complained over. Further examination of the situation often revealed that the dissention was caused not by the assumed maligner, but by subtle hostility from the accuser. As a woman in the professional engineering and architecture world for many years, I never had a problem [with] asserting my authority or education. [I'm] Not saying I never experienced folks trying to be condescending; just that I had the wherewithal to deflect and ignore, and, in most cases, deal with them swiftly, on my own, without having to bring in upper management or coming down to their level. Just my view, but the women who succeed don't need peer or family approval; don't spend time seeking accolades, and certainly know how to use every and any available resource to ensure their success! So now, as a small business owner, my success is on my own shoulders: my success is due to endurance, patience, strength, planning, and strategizing. I am not a victim of my color, but a woman on a mission. [I] Have never used my ethnicity as an excuse for failure; the fault would be mine for letting it affect me, not theirs for their ignorance. [There are] Too many opportunities in this day and age to point the finger, [so it's] time to accept what is, overcome, and find another way. When things don't work out, I hit the ground running and move on to the next part of the plan. Opportunities abound.

—Jeanette, NC

Pay it Forward

I can find no better way to close this book than to talk about BossLadyShip and paying it forward. This is such a hallmark of leadership. I started the book with the story of how my own leadership journey began at college, trying to mediate between those two women. The discussion they were having was an important one: as women (and as women of color), we're standing on the shoulders of the giants who came before us. They paved the way so that we can accomplish the goals and dreams we have for ourselves today. As we accomplish, so, too, must we pay it forward to the BabyBossLadies out there.

- **Mentor.** We've discussed in previous chapters how women feel about mentoring other BossLadies. There's always value in helping groom the next generation of leaders and entrepreneurs, so find a woman who you're compatible with; who has the smarts, drive, and passion to be successful at what she puts her mind to. Ensure she wants what you're willing to mentor her to achieving.

- **Give advice.** Advice is also part of the mentorship process, but there are many women who'll ask for your advice or your opinion on a myriad of issues. This is a double-edged sword: sometimes, you need to be honest and let that woman know that what she wants or where she is heading is not in the best interest of her ultimate goals. Correcting trajectories is a difficult road, and many people resent—or are at least not receptive or amenable to—that advice. You'll know who those you can be honest with and those you cannot. Honesty is not the same as cruelty, and advice means being honest in a gentle and constructive way so as to bring about learning and growth and not to cut someone off before they've even had an opportunity to bloom.

- **Be a listening ear.** You've learned, through your own journey, how difficult the journey is and can be: it's frustrating, scary, annoying, and joyful, all at the same time. There are a lot of tasks to juggle, people to pacify, clients and customers to satisfy, and emotions to traverse. It's a harrowing process, and sometimes, ladies don't need anyone to tell them what to do; they just need to vent and need a non-judgmental ear as they yell, scream, curse, and sometimes behave in a manner not congruent with the situation. Your job is to be a sympathetic, non-judgmental ear and a broad shoulder for her to lament on.

- **Apprentice.** Years ago, apprenticeships were how people passed on skills and trades—and then came the rise of the degree! Now, however, we're seeing a return in skills attainment: what people want today are those who can get the job done, regardless of whether or not they have a degree. So, if you're a soapmaker, a candlemaker, a baker, or a chef and there are women who respect you and want to learn from you, you're in a position to train those women in your skillset. You'll get help at a reduced cost, knowing your legacy will include creating more professionals, as well as passing on traditions that often get lost when skills training is commercialized.

- **Be supportive.** In addition to being a listening ear, you're also a broad shoulder. Women of color find it difficult to start a business with the capital of other groups; they are often working a 9 to 5 with a side-hustle, until the side-hustle makes enough for it to be their full-time gig. There are many ways we can support other women. We can...
  - o Purchase their product or service at full price.
  - o Refer people to their business.
  - o Help them to build their network.
  - o Refer them to people, groups, or organizations that can help their business or them personally.
  - o Be a helping hand in the business, if needed. Can you be a backup server for your catering BossLady friend? Can you pose for promo pictures, or take pictures for her to post on social media? Can you help her with her children while she attends to an appointment?
  - o Push her business on social media and hashtag her so that she gains better visibility.
- **Be a steward and nurturer of talent.** This is a part of the mentorship practice: when you see a promising and talented BabyBossLady, take her under your wing and

nurture her skills and talent so she can realize her full potential to be a full-fledged BossLady! Encourage her to continue to grow through experience, training, education, and mentorship; encourage her to take on projects that will harness her skill and talent and fine tune it to perfection; encourage her to seek out opportunities for her own self-growth.

Quick points to think about...
- Mentor: What kind of mentorship do you like/want?

_____

_____

_____

- How do you think you can mentor another woman or other women?

_____

_____

_____

- Give advice: What's the best advice another woman ever gave you?

_____

_____

_____

- What's the one thing you would tell a woman who was seeking to be a leader or an entrepreneur?

_____

_____

- Apprentice/Steward of Talent: What areas would you like to be an apprentice in?

_____

_____

_____

- How could you help another woman become an apprentice?

_____

_____

_____

- Be supportive: Supportive Behaviors
  - Purchase their product, refer their business, build their network.
  - Do you know a woman who you can do this for? List her/their names below

_____

_____

_____

Wow! Guess what? We're done!

Just kidding; we're not! We now have a blueprint, so let's go out there and make it happen.

CHAPTER 7:
THE PIVOT

2020: The year the world stopped spinning.

SO, 2020 IS GOING to go down in history as one of the worst years since the 1800s. Why? Well, that's when we first heard the word "Coronavirus"! This isn't a new word; in fact, it's on the side of every Lysol can, but many of us have never ever thought of it. Regardless, here we are in 2020: hostages of an invisible threat.

In February 2020, we began hearing that there was this weird flu out there that seemed to be a little more serious than the bird or swine flu of years prior. Most of us brushed off this new flu, because, come on, thousands of people die each year from the flu, so what's the big deal?

In fact, I got on a plane and headed to Texas for a conference at this time—but as I sat at the airport and saw people in surgical and dust masks, I began to think that maybe this was a little bit more than a seasonal flu. Was I not taking this as seriously as I should be? One of the moms on my son's wrestling team came by to pick up a Wrestling Mom t-shirt the night before I left for my conference, and she insisted that I take a mask, just in case. And this is how, at the beginning of March, I became the proud owner of an N-95 mask.

Nevertheless, undeterred, off I went on the germmobile of an aircraft, to my health education conference in Texas (ironically). Everyone seemed to have a tacit understanding that we really didn't want to be too close to each other. Little did I know that this was my graceful introduction to what we would come to know most intimately as social distancing!

Since this was a conference for health educators, you can well imagine what one of the topics of conversation was. Surrounded by all these seasoned and educated health professionals, I began to realize that this was something serious.

So, now, with more caution, I came back from Texas and immediately go onto my next business trip to Orlando. While there, I was introduced to the Johns Hopkins website that was tracking the COVID-19 cases in the US and worldwide, as well as the mounting death toll. It was then that the reality of the situation hit me, and I realized that this was some serious stuff we were working with.

On that day—March 12th—, I sat with one of my directors and immediately began putting a plan in place for what would happen if this new silent enemy did what it looked like it planned to do. I began scouring the internet, looking at what was happening in Europe and Asia. I realized that the US was operating on borrowed time. With this information under our belts, my director and I began to plan for how our company would continue operating when we were forced to close and operate remotely.

I headed home that Friday and spent the entire weekend working on a strategic plan for finishing the school year and how we would reopen three weeks later using remote technology.

We then spent the week of March 15th figuring out how we were going to make this transition. The first thing we did was create a plan for closing during the term in terms of ensuring that our students could complete finals. By this time, hospitals had suspended our ability to have students on-site for clinical externships. Hospitals refused to take liability for students in what had become epicenters. Our southern locations operated in Dade and Broward counties—the epicenters for the virus in Florida. Next, we figured out which classes need to be moved online, and then how we would pursue virtual classes for our hundreds of students.

Ordinarily, organizations have blueprints for disasters. Operating in Florida, we're quite familiar with hurricanes, so we have huge plans, backups, and contingencies for how to manage a localized disaster such as a hurricane; we didn't, however, have a plan, or even an *idea*, on how to manage a global pandemic. The hallmark of our institution is personalized, in-person, small class environments—and now, we were now looking at a situation where we would have to change our entire business model.

As a business consultant, if I'm asked by a client to help them create a plan to change their business model, we would be looking at a 12- to 18-month transition process. What people pay Dr. Sue Speaks LLC thousands of dollars to engineer, my team and I would now have to accomplish in 10 days—re-engineering your business to meet new market trends. By March 20th, South Florida was put into virtual shutdown, and by March 23rd, we realized that this life of virtual existence with social distancing was our new reality.

From March 22nd all the way to April 6th, I realized I was living in a reality that I had no desire to live in: each day, we watched the worldwide daily infection and death toll rise, and there was little any of us could do to change anything. We then watched as the nation plunged some 40 million people into unemployment, understanding that the economy was about to crash to Great Depression levels. No, not the Great Recession (2008); the Great Depression (1920s). I was literally and physically ill. I retained my job because it was to help keep the wheels of education turning, but I laid off many faculty members as we created new education models and tried to figure out ways to continue to educate students remotely.

On April 6th, we launched our new school term. In 10 days, we had moved hundreds of students online, created new lesson plans to accommodate this new learning modality, and oriented students to this new learning style—but more importantly, we had retained some 75% of our staff. I breathed a sigh of relief and then took a minute to sit back and think about what we had done and all the various organizations we had partnered with, as well as all the new things I'd had to learn in order to make this a reality.

However, on the flipside, I began looking at all my online forums and realized that my reality was not that of many: I had retained my job, and our organization had been successful in getting a Payroll Protection Loan, in turn allowing us to continue paying our staff, even though we had reduced revenue. We'd also received another loan that allowed us to assist our students and pay for the software and technology that fueled and funneled this new reality. I realized that I had written a book based on a reality that no longer existed, and it would take me a few weeks to digest this new reality and figure out the message and lessons I wanted BossLadies to get and learn from what I had learned.

The Story of Lemonade

As part of my Dr. Sue Speaks life, I shoot a weekly video as part of my car video series. As I managed this new business reality, I began to shoot a series of videos I referred to as the Pivot—and I then pivot to making lemonade. The saying is that when life hands you lemons, you make lemonade—so one night, I thought about that and realized how much this aligned with making solid and sound business and personal decisions.

So, let's think about it. How do you make lemonade?

1. You have lemons, which are inherently sour, but have great benefits from health to sanitizing to overall wellness.

2. You need a jug.
3. You need a spoon.
4. You need a sweetening agent.

I do a really awesome job of explaining this in my video, so if you're someone who likes to hear and see things, go take a minute and view it. It's a great watch!

So, in order to make the lemonade, there are steps you are going to need to follow:

1. You're going to need to tolerate the sour, because the current reality is the current reality; there is absolutely *nothing* we can do to change this. Instead, we have to find ways to mitigate the situation and essentially tolerate the sour. So, how do we do that?

2. We need to get a jug and a spoon. Well, what are those? Those are our tools; the things we're going to use to stir the lemonade in order for it to become more palatable to us.

3. We need a sweetener. We can use sugar, Splenda, Stevia, Honey... The choice is ours.

Essentially, we're finding tools to use that will help us make a sour/intolerable situation one that is not only more tolerable, but also somewhat enjoyable to manage and/or drink. This is essentially the Pivot: it's all of us figuring out the tools we are going to use to navigate our way to a new reality both during and post COVID-19.

Corona Changed the Workplace

For many years, many organizations were adamant they couldn't operate with remote employees; however, what we discovered was that this was clearly false. In April of 2020, many organizations sent their staff home with computers, software, VPNs, and a host of tools that allowed them to work remotely. It's yet to be seen how this going to eventually change when offices are allowed to bring staff back into buildings, but COVID is expected to be a part of our landscape until sometime in 2022. What changes this will create long-term are still to be seen; however, we *do* already know that many employees are beginning to question the need to work in organizations that "require" them to be present to measure productivity when they were being productive in absentia.

So, was it really that employees "needed" to be present within a building to be productive? Or was it that organizations felt they needed to monitor staff in order to ensure productivity? The latter is a sad commentary, as it states two things: an inherent belief that staff are lazy; and an organization's inability to choose self-motivated, driven, and productive staff. We do know that many BossLadies have left their jobs because of both of those organizational beliefs, so this can't be completely without merit!

The Corporate BossLady

How does this new reality impact the BossLady? That is still to be seen, but here is what is mission-critical: as a BossLady, your new mission will be to be constantly vigilant and watchful over what's happening within the organization; measuring the temperature of the corporate, executive, management, and staff to determine what is happening and what your actions will be. The sand is shifting in corporate America, and where it will settle is anyone's guess; however, what I say to the BossLady is that your job is to be vigilant and then take advantage of whatever will work for you when it comes. I would advise you to keep a variety of sweeteners and stirring utensils to be ready to implement within the jug of lemonade you'll be mixing in the next 18 months!

The Entrepreneur BossLady

This has not been fun for those BossLadies who created their businesses following every single piece of advice given, only to watch business and revenue dry up as the country ground to a halt in mid-March! Then, when they were trying to get loans from the SBA, they found they'd been cheated by large organizations who'd snapped up the resources that were meant to help them keep their businesses alive and afloat. As an entrepreneur myself, my business is about doing group trainings, and now, those trainings are no longer allowed as a result of social distancing measures. I fully agree with such action, but I also quickly began to worry about how I was supposed to have a six-figure year if my business model was no longer allowed. I watched everyone moving to virtual training and creating masterclasses, and I realized that a model that I'd thought was something that was a "future" thing was now the only way I was going to be able to sustain my own business: for me, I had to get the jug going to add the sugar of a masterclass to my business mix.

But this wasn't going to work for everyone: many BossLadies had created businesses that were about personal services (e.g., makeup; hair; exercise; massages), and focused on a personal one-on-one experience—which was now something they were told was high-risk, and that they couldn't indulge in making a living or building their empires. Now, this invisible invader had rendered them inoperable, with no idea of when things would return to normal.

Dr. Sue Speaks LLC and @SocialwithLulu had planned the Like A Boss Conference, to be held in South Florida, in September of 2020. As of the writing this chapter in June of 2020, we have no plans to actually hold the conference: the number of infections are beginning to rise, and the state has not permitted people to meet in groups larger than 50. Hence, the hallmark of #WomenSupportingWomen, which was in-person groups and meetups, had suddenly come to a halt. Thus came the rise of Zoom, a non-US based conferencing company that literally took the entire world by storm: conferences, birthdays, school, and all virtual learning began to happen on Zoom. The notion of large groups meeting to share became antithetical to health and something that nobody was willing to discuss. Instead, everyone had chosen the virtual route.

And, while the hallmark of being a BossLady is having and plan and having a backup (and, yes, even a contingency), it seemed near impossible to even *think* of a plan to create: the level of uncertainty was just too high. Everyone was trying desperately to simply return to their basic lives, focused on trying to find toilet paper and hand sanitizer, re-learning proper hand washing techniques, thinking about living one's best life, and helping others to level up.

The New Normal

In my own business, I began to focus on creating weekly videos aimed at helping everyone through this new normal. These were the Pivot car video series: I was trying to help my public recognize that the past and yesterday was just that— the past! Nothing was going to return "as we knew it", so the first thing that we had to confront was that the economy had tanked. When 40 million people are out of work and unemployment is approaching 15%, people don't have discretionary income; instead, people are focused on the immediate and necessary—what financial Guru Dave Ramsey refers to as the Four Walls: shelter, food, transportation, and utilities. So, if this is the new normal, what's a BossLady to do?

The Pivot

So, I've talked about the Pivot, but what did this really mean? It meant exactly what it says: everybody was going to have to literally spin around and figure out how to make this virus, which was currently haunting us, a part of our daily existence by respecting its ferocity and figuring out how to continue and thrive while simultaneously keeping it at bay. "Pivot" was the new word for adapting to chance. This is not new: BossLadies have been doing this forever. For BossLadies of color, this is the norm and essentially how many of our businesses came into being—but now, the virus and its fallout were creating a need for us to find an additional Pivot related to a new mode of delivery for success.

What do I mean by this? Well, I like watching *90 Day Fiancé* on TLC, and one of the former participants, Molly Hopkins, owns LiviRae, a bra business in Atlanta. When the country closed and stores had to close up shop, she, too, had to close up shop; however, through sheer serendipity, she saw a man who was using a bra as a face mask. She suddenly realized she could create face masks (our new fashion and health accessory) because a) she had the raw materials, and b) she had the know-how. So, she and her business partner, Cynthia Decker, began creating masks for sale and distribution while also using videos to continue her core business virtually. Now, not only did she continue her core business using a new modality (Zoom video), but she also expanded her business blueprint. Excellent BossLadyship, Molly and Cynthia!

This is the Pivot: looking at your current reality and finding how you can use your expertise and materials to create a new business and revenue stream. The POTUS has the ability to require organizations to change their business and create whatever the country needs produced for the good of the country, so a BossLady will need to look at what the emerging and hitherto unknown needs of the marketplace are and then determine how her business will Pivot to fill the gap. Then, BossLadies of color will need to find those niches that are still *not* being filled and ensure to fill those, creating unique niches. There are some people who have a gift for this: they're able to rise above the fray and see things from a 30-foot height and predict where the market will go, and so position themselves to be there just in the nick of time. Others need to stay with the current stream and see how the flow is meandering and then align their goals and plans with the new flow.

The mask business is one which many have Pivoted: we, in the United States, have always snickered at the Chinese for wearing masks for years, and yet in an attempt to try to create some level of normalcy, many of us are accepting that face masks are going to be a way of life for the foreseeable future. People have created a variety of masks to meet the ergonomic needs of many: there are now masks for people involved in sports, which have a greater level of breathability, and designers and fashionistas have created masks to not only go with every outfit, but to also serve as branding for businesses. I recently went into a restaurant to pick up my dinner and realized that all the staff were wearing the same stylish black masks to match their uniforms. Six months ago, who would have thought that masks would be as essential to our daily lives as our cellphones?

@cakeitmiami is another BossLady who did a huge Pivot: I was turned on to this BossLady by Lulu, as we would share stories of BossLadies Pivoting in our nightly WhatsApp chat sessions. We were essentially trying to convince one of our BabyBossLadies to take the plunge of the Pivot herself. @cakeitmiami is a local bakery in Miami, and, with the Corona lockdown and with Miami-Dade being the epicenter of the pandemic in Florida, the county was under lockdown. However, restaurants could do limited business with delivery, pickup, and curbside service—and @cakeitmiami took this to a higher level. She created at-home cake kits that had all the ingredients to bake and decorate a cake. With children at home with parents, she had created the perfect DIY kit; then, she did IG Lives, where she taught people how to use the kits they would buy.

One night, I found myself glued to her live video as I watched her create a unicorn cake; then, while she did this, she engaged with her audience and donated the cake to someone who answered a question correctly on the live. She's a living testimony to someone who did a Pivot to keep her business alive during a change in economic times.

There are, I'm sure, millions of stories of BossLadies who did the Pivot and stayed in business in the midst of the economic crisis that leveled the US in April 2020. I noticed that BossLadies of color were creating fun t-shirts to sell, promoting ethnic heritage and pride during lockdown. The closure of hair salons meant that BossLadies who had leveled up to create products now had an even greater market: for some three months, salons were closed, forcing many women to purchase products and do their own hair at home. Taraji P. Henson could be seen using her own products on Instagram and sharing with likely customers the outcome of the products on her own hair!

Business pundits have stated that many small businesses have closed and are unlikely to reopen, and, if this is true, this is a devastating fact: in 2020, Guidant Financial reported that 27% of small businesses were owned by women. This therefore suggests that BossLadies have been severely impacted by the COVID-19 epidemic as small business owners—and, while this may sound like a small number, in 2019, the National Association of Women Business Owners stated that there are some 11 million female entrepreneurs. That is a *staggering* number! We really won't know the impact of COVID-19 on small businesses, and then women, and then women of color, until well in 2021. This is because many are still waiting for some level of normalcy to see how they will survive toward the end of 2020 and into 2021.

The goal of this book has been to help women harness their own power to become BossLadies, either in the organization in which they work, or to become an entrepreneur. Now, those principles don't fundamentally change; what *will* change, however, is *how* BossLadies can execute those principles when we're experiencing a higher-than-normal level of unemployment.

This, however, is not the time to despair: the one thing we know is that when things are down, the only way out is up! Hence, now is the time for some serious introspection, taking all the lessons learned earlier in this book, and putting those things into play to determine what your new direction will be. As I keep saying in my Dr. Sue car videos, I'm not quite sure *how* I will do a full Pivot, but I'm looking into what that should be. This is going to be a work in progress, so keep watching my Instagram while we work through this new reality together and exit, triumphant, on the other side!

Steps to the Pivot

1. What is my core business?
2. Are there now new avenues that I can explore?
3. How does my business benefit the client? Are their new clients that I can now gain?
4. Are there benefits that I did not look into or did not wish to pursue before?

5. How can I now take advantage of that thing I didn't wish to pursue before?
6. What are other BossLadies doing?
7. What can I learn from them?
8. What new things do I need to learn?
9. What comfort zone circle am I in? (Now is not the time for the comfort zone; BossLadyship doesn't live here!)
   - The Fear Zone is very real, so allow yourself to feel the fear. However, don't live there: again, BossLadyship doesn't live there! We need to fear *being* there, because death occurs there.
   - The Learning Zone is a great place for BossLadies right now. There's a lot going on, and everyone is talking about #TheNewNormal, but no one really knows what that is yet. Where most of us are living in 2020 is what's important until we figure out what happens after we get over COVID-19.
   - What is "after" exactly, anyway? "After" is the reality that we'll be existing in, come 2021; it's knowing and understanding that it'll be dissimilar to what February of 2020 looked like, and BossLadies will (and must) adjust—whether that means less travelling (replaced with the implantation of more virtual meetings), the existence of facemasks as both a necessity, fashion statement, and marketing strategy, or the expansion of a virtual reality to augment a physical existence.

○ The Growth Zone is ultimately what the Pivot is about: it's about moving through the learning zone and then emerging *after* with clarity and focus, understanding the new market and then making decisions on how you will begin to build the empire of your choosing.

Understanding the Marketplace and Current Trends

COVID-19 has shifted the entire US economy. What had been up until April a booming economy came crashing down as the country sheltered in place in order to reduce the impact of illness on the healthcare system, as well as to lower the death toll. Over 40 million people would become unemployed; the 3.8% unemployment rate would balloon to 14%+; and it would become almost impossible to determine what the marketplace even was. The measures of job numbers, the stock market, and consumer spending would become moot points to determine economic health. We'd been hearing economists talk about a recession, but nobody had anticipated this entire collapse as businesses closed, especially small business, which are the backbone of the US economy.

The government would pour billions into the economy in an attempt to ensure there would not be as much damage as there could be. Payroll loans were made; small business loans were given out; unemployment payments were increased. The goal was to keep people from becoming homeless or starving to death, and ensuring that small businesses would survive the devastation of the pandemic. However, again, the inequities were glaring and obvious: CBS News, on April 22nd, 2020, would state that some 90% of minority and female owners were shut out of the Payroll Protection Program. It was then found that many of the minority-owned businesses did not benefit from the first round of the PPP loans. It wasn't until those funds were given to community banks, credit unions, and community development financial institutions that BossLadies of color would see some funds for their businesses.

Many BossLadies of color said the standards for the loans were so onerous and difficult to understand that it made more sense for those who *did* get the loans to actually return them. One BossLady I know, who owns a Salon Suite and has seven other ladies who rent from her, is still pondering if (and how) to use the loan. She's decided to keep the money as a cushion and to repay it as a loan as necessary; having worked tirelessly to get the loan, the notion of giving it back when it could be useful at a later date seemed counterproductive to success.

The thing to keeping #BossLadyship is first creating the Pivot for you and your organization for reality, and then understanding the public in a post-COVID reality. COVID has changed everyone, so there are a number of groups and demographics that need to be considered as you contemplate your Pivot. Each of these groups will now think and behave differently, and you, as you create your new reality, will need to take this new behavior into account.

- **Parents**. Parents will now have a much greater appreciation for educators, having spent three months engaged in virtual education of their children. As an educator myself and a friend to many who are in the K-12 system, I speak on their behalf in hoping that everyone now understands that teaching is an honorable profession, and teachers are not dumb, stupid, incompetent, or lazy—an accusation leveled at many prior to COVID-19. Today, they are recognized as the vital linchpins they are in our society and economy. This becomes an asset if you're working in any type of education, mentorship, coaching, or teaching field, as parents are more likely to pay and invest more: they understand the value of education. On the flipside, other parents have now experienced virtual education, and are now seeing the value of this, having had to dive in headfirst. They're now more likely to homeschool their children, since they have now seen how well their children adapt to this. How does this then impact your business? How do you now connect with these parents if you have a business that requires you to connect with these groups? Or, if you're thinking of expanding an education-based business, what kind of support can you offer to working parents now embarking upon the online or virtual chooling of their children?
- **Employers**. For years, employers have espoused the notion that staff had to be all together within the confines of a building in order for a business to ensure

productivity. This notion that people had to be in a building to perform was severely challenged during COVID-19, as employers sent their staff members home *en masse* and realized that their business continued quite successfully without staff being in the same building. Virtual meeting software (e.g., Zoom, GOTO, and WebEx) became the standard means for businesses to continue their meetings, as well as business transactions. Instead of business people flying around the globe, they sat at their dining tables or in their offices and continued to cut deals, and the wheels of commerce kept turning. Now, companies are rethinking their ways of doing things: some organizations are now choosing to have employees remain remote, as they've seen the success of what remote work could mean, as well as how the reduction in overheads could impact their businesses positively. Some organizations, similarly, are rethinking the need to have their staff constantly flying and staying in hotels for meetings that can essentially be held by Skype. So, as a #BossLady, how are you going to benefit from this shift? This might work well for you, especially if you're working within an organization.

- **Benefits**. There were two things that happened during the shelter-in-place process: many #BossLady moms had the joy of spending more time with their children. I was one of them: my son is 17, and sometimes, his life as an academic and wrestler was so busy that I felt we were ships in the night. My marriage would end during the pandemic, and by the time I was working from home, my husband had already moved out. That left me with my son. I found that working from home allowed me to not only work longer hours and get more done, since I'd removed the commute from the equation, but that my son and I were always together: we shared coffee in the morning, joint lunches, and joint dinners. What I thought would be a giant issue actually ended up being a great thing: he became my official photographer and spent lots of time giving me ideas for videos as I tried to figure out the world of the Pivot.

- **The Public**. In March of 2020, the public had some very clear expectations of companies. By June of 2020, those expectations would be vastly different: not only were patrons wondering about company's cleaning protocols, social distancing standards, and mask-wearing requirements, but after a police officer made a very wrong decision, patrons now started looking at the social policies of organizations to determine how and where they would be spending their money and which organizations they would support. In June of 2020, the public leveraged their collective bargaining power and took to the street, Twitter, TikTok, and a variety of social media vehicles to let companies know exactly what they would and would not support. Some business owners found themselves ostracized and/or blackballed; some BossLadies who held some antiquated societal standards found their business abandoned, or their companies firing them for not meeting the socially acceptable new norms expected in June of 2020; other #BossLadies discovered they could use their voices to become social justice warriors and used TikTok as a medium to garner support and awareness for their cause.

- **Your client**. Because I was social distancing, there is just so much Netflix that you can watch before needing a new outlet! My new outlet is TikTok: I post nothing; instead, I am a stalker. Initially, I watched to see all the new dance crazes, but then, at the end of May, the vibe on TikTok moved to one of social justice vs entertainment—and many BossLadies who were experiencing personal and financial backlash from taking socially new positions found that the conservative norms were forcing them to make a stand. And they did! They used their 60 seconds on TikTok to make clear, definitive statements about their brand and what they would and would not accept. Many of these women were Millennials and Gen X, and what this signaled was a distinct shift in the mindset of the new #BossLady—especially those of color. No longer would they accept anything less than full inclusion, but, more importantly, they were willing to take this stand even if it meant losing clients. The goal during this time would be for like-minded BossLadies and clients to find each other, even if it meant crossing state lines to do so.

Maintaining your #BossLadyship Post-COVID-19

Now, as we look to close this chapter, here's what to think about and to actively put in place:

1. **You're a queen,** so adjust your crown! You've got this!
2. **Be flexible!** Understand that the ground is still shifting. Things are never going to be the same and everyone is uncertain about the future, but be open to change and moving in new directions: the one thing you do know is that change is inevitable!
3. **The Pivot.** The flexibility you adopt will allow you to Pivot! As changes are occurring and you see an unfilled niche that you think you can fill, by all means, move forward positively to fill that niche.
4. **Advantages.** Remember to look at your advantages with new eyes: the environment is different; the market is different; your old advantages may no longer be necessary. If you're used to planning thousand-person conferences, shift that to how you can do this remotely with the same level of success, knowing that it'll be well into 2022 before large conferences will begin to draw the same kinds of crowds! The public will be wary of large groups for a while.

5. **Finances.** Where are you? How stable are you? Now may be the time to invest in meeting with a financial planner so that you're definitely creating a safe financial future for yourself. Investment portfolios took a hit in 2020, and will take a minute to recover, so that's something you need to think of.

6. **Revenue stream.** With 20 million people unemployed, you'll now need to determine where there is revenue for your business. There are some questions that you'll need to ask yourself and then determine the answers to in order to move forward. Do you need to rethink your business for a while? Are you liquid enough with your business to be able to survive an income shortfall over the next few months? If you are, carry on. If you're not, then should you perhaps seek short-term employment so that you have a consistent income while you rebuild your clientele and ability to be a self-sustaining BossLady.

Now, you could be one of those #BossLadies who found a niche during the pandemic and are doing very well—and if that is you, then well done! Please remember to pay it forward and teach another BossLady how to replicate your success. However, if you've found that you've needed to rethink your strategy, then don't despair: this is not the end; this is simply you reassessing how you'll get to your final goal.

So, what does this all mean? Quite simply, it means that #BossLadies will need to create a new reality and find new levels of balance for this reality. This entire book has discussed this relationship women of color have with balance: there are expectations of them being able to "do it all with a

smile" that will need to be addressed by each person so as to determine just how much adaptation they will need to do personally in order to embrace their new reality and find some level of comfort and then success. The first seven chapters of this book discussed how to create a balance to achieve BossLadyship pre-COVID-19; now, a new reality will need to be created, and #BossLadies across the globe will be creating this new reality together.

CHAPTER 8:
MAY 25, 2020 —
THE DAY WHEN PEOPLE
BECAME WOKE AND ALLIES

I N THE PREVIOUS CHAPTER, I talked about my TikTok addiction. Look, no judging! I spend at least two hours on TikTok each night listening to these 60-second snippets of greatness. This was the medium which gave me hope: staying at home and social distancing meant that I didn't get to be out there in the world seeing what was happening, but TikTok allowed #BossLadies of color to realize the world was changing. We had allies!

On February 23rd, a young man went jogging in Georgia. His name was Ahmaud Arbery. He would never return home from that run: he was chased down by three white men and murdered on the street. One of those men would capture that murder on his cellphone camera and get it to the police. Then, on March 13th, 2020, a young EMT, home from battling COVID-19, would be killed in a no-knock raid. Her name was Breona Taylor. The world was paralyzed by COVID-19, and I was still trying to figure out how I was going to create a Pivot and write this chapter in order to help women find their BossLadyship. These two incidents were literally buried under the weight of a global pandemic.

However, in a few weeks, both names would become household names. When Ahmaud's story was unleashed months after his death, people became incensed: Corona had people home with nothing to do, so they had sit—to *really* sit—and listen to this young man's story and begin to think about a world that exists with disparity for people who are not a part of the majority. Then, when people realized that a young EMT fighting COVID had also faced a similar violent death, there was a swelling of annoyance that began to bubble up. When people have no distractions and are trapped at home, there needs to be an outlet.

So, on May 25th, the world was poised to erupt—but we couldn't even fathom that a single event would literally shift the trajectory of history. On May 25th, George Floyd was murdered by a Minneapolis police officer. A 17-year-old young lady of color, Darnella Frazier, would record Mr. Floyd's death—the eight minutes and 46 seconds of police officer Chauvin's knee on George's neck, eventually leading to his death by asphyxiation. Cabin fever, exhaustion, exasperation, unemployment, contempt for how the COVID-19 crisis was handled, and general malaise over the situation in the country erupted like a geyser: within days, an entire movement had

begun around the world. #GeorgeFloyd became the hashtag that everyone associated with.

Millions of people in stark defiance of social distancing began taking to the streets. Some protests got violent, with bad actors trying to change the narrative; but then, something amazing began happening. People of different ages, races, socioeconomic backgrounds, and faiths began to stand up and say, "Enough is enough." What began as a protest against police brutality morphed into a resurgence of the #BLM movement, with an understanding that systemic racism has been engineered to keep an entire race of people under the thumb of the white majority, and that it was time to break the system.

Was This the Real Pivot?

1. We watch the Amish come out in support of ending brutality against people of color.
2. We watch millennials decide that this is not what they stand for and will fight, march, and protest to create change.
3. We watch Generation Z challenge their parents on TikTok not to the latest dance challenge, but to change their long-held opinions about people of color.
4. We watch as Cuban-Americans challenge other Cuban-Americans to change their opinion about other people of color.

5. We watch as the LGBTQIA+ community challenge those who remained quiet and were not protesting that it was a black woman, Marsha P. Johnson, to whom they owe Stonewall and the eventual Pride movement.
6. We watch as the Wiccan community comes out in support of the #BLM movement, and—wait for it!—as they are supported by the Christian community, praying for them as they cast spells of positivity for the #BlackLivesMatter movement.
7. We watch as the term "ally" became a hashtag all over TikTok as we watch this new normal emerge.

As a woman of color, I've always understood that the reason we had to be different was because the majority didn't really understand that we lived in two different worlds. Not only did they not understand the reality of their sisters of color, but they had little interest in understanding that reality. In 2016, with new leadership in the country, the ugly underbelly of racism and refusal to be understanding of others rose up to the forefront. The good thing about this is that nobody had to wonder if people were racist or intolerant of others: they made it very clear that they were! However, as the world watched the death of George Floyd, it flipped a switch in humanity.

Many white people, with nothing to distract them, watching as a man died in broad daylight, were stunned into a reality that their current normal essentially meant metaphorically keeping their knees in the backs of people of color. We would watch as people pledged to listen, learn, and do better. Many racists didn't really understand that the shift came out with their normal rhetoric, and found that the new normal was not pleasant to them: not only were they ridiculed on social media, but many found themselves unemployed as organizations raced to distance themselves from anyone not aligned to the #BlackLivesMatter movement.

As a businesswoman, mentor, public speaker, author, and coach, I had to stop and think, *What does this mean for me?* In the previous chapter, I discussed all the various steps in the Pivot; in April my thoughts on the Pivot bore very little resemblance to what I'm now thinking in June. In June, I'm realizing that the world has shifted on its axis: the white people who comprise some 45% of the US population are now becoming more and more open to changing the way they do things in order to give more access to #BossLadiesOfColor. This was highlighted on Instagram, when white women of renown and influence gave their IG platforms over to black women in order for them to have access to their followers and spread their messages.

So, how will this impact BossLadyship? I don't know how each BossLady will need to change, but I look at myself and realize that my greatest asset to the #BlackLivesMatter movement and being part of the Pivot is to become an agent of change. Remember that term? It's something that women of color are already familiar with being. I need to take my skills of compromise and negotiation and help individuals and groups figure out how they can change their current reality, practices, beliefs, and actions to create a new reality that will be more beneficial to helping more women of color achieve #BossLadyship.

So, I'm now going to end this book on June 15th, 2020, the date of this final entry. I know that by the time this book is in the hands of my readers, things will be vastly different; my hope is that our allies have stood with us and that we have convinced more and more people to create an equalization, so that while #BossLadies have a different culture, that no longer precludes them from having the same access to power, wealth, and advantage that their white allies enjoy.

ACKNOWLEDGEMENTS

WHEN I FIRST STARTED writing this book, I had no idea where I would be when the time came for the book to finally be published. I started in December 2019, and now, in the fall of 2020—almost a year later—, so much in my life has changed. With this in mind, I feel a need to acknowledge all the women and people who have helped me get to this milestone.

My journey from this time last year to now has been a story involving so many queens, all of which who have regularly helped me to adjust my own crown. Any major life change requires a support system, and I've been lucky enough to have a stellar one! As a woman of faith, I was awed at His moving them into my life just as I needed them.

Without further ado:

To Tresia Anne Rose, who always reminded me to take it to Him.

To Julie Ann Smith, my ride-or-die, who reminded me that a resting bitch face is never an option, and whose recommendations were always spot on.

To Liezette Abel-Ruffin, who always lends a willing ear and a guiding presence.

To Shondra Saunders Russell, who for months has checked in on me on the daily.

To Nicole "Nickie Nix" Evans, my BFF who always tries to keep me reasonable and grounded.

To Winston Buddle, who has been there for 30 years: my man of honor, who has always been there as a true friend.

To Carolyn Lewis, who reminded me that who I am is awesome, and needs no apologies.

To Bridgette Reid, who has known me the longest, confirmed that I was as Michelle Obama, and said that I was becoming the best version of me.

To Michelle Byfield, who just supported me because, in her words, I'm her sister.

To Jean Crawford and Germaine Rogers-Smith, for that awesome Valentine's dinner and the great advice.

To Lourdes Amador (Lulu), my student-turned-friend, coworker, and business partner, who told me to stop hiding my light. Dr. Sue Speaks LLC exists because you didn't stop until it did!

To Debbie Jones, for making me focus on the practical.

And special thanks to two people who have literally crafted the woman I am today: the first, my mom, Sonia. It pains me that even though you're here with us physically, you're not seeing the manifestation of your greatest life achievement—me!—become everything you desired and wanted for me from birth.

The second is my son and light of my heart, Tristan. You gave me a reason to want to be bigger and better.